BILL CLARKE

Marketing for the Small Business in Ireland

GILL AND MACMILLAN

Published in Ireland by
Gill and Macmillan Ltd
Goldenbridge
Dublin 8
with associated companies in
Auckland, Delhi, Gaborone, Hamburg, Harare,
Hong Kong, Johannesburg, Kuala Lumpur, Lagos, London,
Manzini, Melbourne, Mexico City, Nairobi,
New York, Singapore, Tokyo
© Bill Clarke 1990
0 7171 1686 7
Print origination by
Seton Music Graphics Ltd, Bantry, Co. Cork
Printed by
Billing & Sons Ltd, Worcester

All rights reserved. No part of this publication may be copied,
reproduced or transmitted in any form or by any means,
without permission of the publishers.

Contents

	Introduction	
1.	What is Marketing Anyway?	1
2.	Defining Your Market	11
3.	Doing Market Research	23
4.	Deciding What to Sell	44
5.	Setting a Price	61
6.	Organising Distribution	78
7.	Contacting the Customer	100
8.	Advertising	121
9.	Selling	143
10.	Sales Management	157
11.	Developing a Marketing Strategy	172
12.	Drawing up a Marketing Plan	183
13.	The Way Ahead	193
	Index	196

Introduction

It is often alleged that small firms in Ireland, both North and South, are not very good at marketing. The truth of the matter is that quite a few of them display a very high level of marketing expertise. On the whole, however, these tend to be the exceptions rather than the rule. Perhaps a better way of describing the overall average level of performance would be to use the phrase sometimes encountered in end-of-term school reports — 'Tries hard, but could do better'.

Unfortunately, when people who actually manage small businesses make an effort to improve their marketing skills, they are all too often swamped by an intensive barrage of technical jargon. Somehow it seems that experts in every field feel compelled to invent a new and complicated language to explain things that are really very simple to understand. Maybe it is a way of protecting their 'expertise', or of justifying their fees.

Another problem is that most of the books currently available which deal with marketing are written on the assumption that they will be read by people working in a large company with substantial resources and a separate marketing department. Such books do not often take into account the constraints faced by small firms located in a peripheral region of Europe. Again, it is at once both amusing and annoying to sit through a marketing 'workshop' organised for the owners and managers of small businesses and to watch them switch off one by one while a marketing 'expert' rambles on in a language which is incomprehensible to most of them, using examples which are totally irrelevant to their needs.

This book sets out to do two things. First, it aims to adapt and apply the fundamentals of marketing theory to the real world of the average small business in Ireland. Secondly, it explains the basic principles in terms which the average manager of a small business can understand and apply to his or her own situation.

You must be the judge of whether or not these objectives have been achieved.

Bill Clarke
University of Ulster

1.
What is Marketing Anyway?

Just about everyone who is trying to manage a small business today must be aware of the need for effective marketing in order to ensure short-term profitability and long-term survival. Government ministers, senior officials and civil servants, business consultants and academics — they all seem to go out of their way to make that basic point on every conceivable occasion. The trouble is that they rarely go on to tell you exactly what they mean by improving your marketing, and how you should go about it. The situation is not helped by the fact that many managers in smaller firms are not entirely clear in their own minds about what effective marketing actually means in terms of running their business from day to day. A useful starting point in sorting out this confusion is to remember that the term *marketing* is used in two quite separate ways:

- To describe a basic mental attitude to the problems of running the business as a whole; and
- As a convenient bit of shorthand to cover a number of quite different but closely related activities which, taken together, are referred to as marketing.

MARKETING AS A PHILOSOPHY OF BUSINESS

There are basically two ways in which you can think about how you run your business. You can be:

- PRODUCT ORIENTED
  or
- MARKET ORIENTED

If you are product oriented, most of your thinking and actions will be dominated by what is happening inside the business. You will be primarily concerned with ensuring that the product or service you offer is of good quality, produced efficiently at the minimum possible cost, that deliveries go out on time, and that customers are promptly and correctly invoiced for their purchases. It would be naive to suggest that there is anything wrong with paying close attention to all of these facets of your business. But you must also realise that the world outside your own premises is constantly changing. Indeed, the pace of change seems to be accelerating all the time. Existing and potential customers are being influenced continuously from so many different directions. It is very unlikely that they will be entirely satisfied now with exactly the same product or level of service as they were offered five years ago, or even eighteen months ago. Their tastes, opinions and buying habits will almost certainly have changed.

The unavoidable fact that markets are constantly changing is possibly the most important single lesson you can learn about marketing. What you must do about it is to shift the focus of your attention from what is happening inside the firm to what is happening outside it in the markets you seek to serve. You must make an effort to find out in detail exactly what your customers want. You must then set out to provide a product or service which meets their needs better than any of the alternatives offered by your competitors. This is what is meant by being market oriented. The product oriented manager makes something and then lifts his or her head from the work-bench to look around the world to see who he or she might persuade to buy it. Market oriented managers reverse the sequence — they first look at the needs of their customers and then try to provide what is required to satisfy them.

There was a time, not really all that long ago, when firms could afford to be product oriented. You may have come across the famous remark attributed to Henry Ford — the people who bought his cars could have 'any colour they like, so long as it's black'. That strategy was possible in the 1920s, when the demand for cars was far greater than the total number of cars being offered for sale. It can still work even today in closed economies where demand exceeds supply — for example in the Soviet Union, where it seems that people are more than happy to be given the opportunity to buy what most of us in the West would regard as a poor quality copy of an obsolete Fiat. Even in the prosperous Western world, it sometimes happens that the current level of demand for a particular product or service is not being met, for one reason or another. In all of these situations, there is really no need to bother too much about the detail of marketing — an effective distribution system is all that is required to dispose of total output and earn substantial profits.

Unfortunately for most firms most of the time, the world simply isn't like that any more. The normal scenario is that supply exceeds demand. In other words, the amount of a particular product or service offered for sale is substantially more than the amount which customers wish to buy.

Even in the case of temporary shortages, you can rest assured that as soon as the excess demand is noticed, somebody, somewhere, will devote a lot of time and energy to increasing their output, or finding an alternative source from which they can import an acceptable substitute. In the modern, industrialised Western world, potential customers are offered an enormously wide range of competing goods and services. They make their choices about what to buy on the basis of factors other than simple availability — design, style, brand image, price, quality, reliability and so on. The facts of the matter are really very simple. It is no longer relevant to ask yourself whether or not you should be market oriented — you simply cannot afford not to be.

Of course, adopting marketing as the basis of your thinking and planning does *not* mean that you neglect the other areas of your business. Obviously you must continue to aim at providing a good-quality product or service as efficiently as possible. But you cannot avoid this basic fact of life — the only reason you survive in business is because your customers believe that what you provide for them meets their needs. If they start to believe that someone else can satisfy their needs better than you can, then you are finished — and no amount of clever manoeuvring or astute financial management will save you.

THE ACTIVITIES INVOLVED IN MARKETING

Many people are confused by the supposed distinction between marketing and sales. At one extreme, there is the view that marketing is simply a fancy word for selling, and there is nothing more to it than that. At the other extreme, marketing and selling are regarded as quite separate and unrelated activities. This situation sometimes arises in bigger companies which can afford the luxury of having both a Sales Manager and a Marketing Manager, who quite often don't work as closely together as they should.

Another source of confusion is that there are now quite a lot of organisations of various kinds which clearly and obviously engage in quite sophisticated marketing, but don't actually sell anything. Examples include government departments trying to convince us all not to smoke, to drink less, to drive carefully and to avoid catching AIDS; or charities trying to persuade us to contribute to famine relief in the Third World.

If you are running a small business which makes a product or provides a service which you sell in order to make a profit, the problem simply does not arise. The whole point of your marketing activity is to maximise your sales.

SELLING IS PART OF MARKETING.

Successful selling is the end product of your total marketing effort — but effective marketing involves a lot more than selling. Think for a moment about what you would need to do to really apply the marketing philosophy in your business.

If you are to be truly customer oriented, you would need to find out as much as you can about your potential customers. How many of them are there? Where are they located? What are their buying habits? You would also need to know as much as possible about the activities of your competitors, and about the general business environment within which you operate. In other words, you need to do some *market research*.

There is not much point in doing market research unless you apply the lesson it provides. You may discover that your product or service is not as highly regarded in the marketplace as you thought it was, or that it compares unfavourably with the offerings of your competitors. It may be out-of-date, or over-priced, or maybe even under-priced. You may notice a gap in the market which you could fill with a new product or service. The key point to remember is that decisions about what *products* you are going to offer, and what *prices* you are going to charge, are *marketing* decisions.

You must also make sure that every potential customer is aware of your existence, and of what you have to offer them. *Advertising* is the most obvious way of achieving this, but it can be expensive and beyond the reach of the smaller firm. Remember that direct media advertising is not the only means available to you for communicating effectively with potential customers and for presenting your product or service to them in an attractive way which will persuade them to buy it. The alternatives include:

- *Publicity material* — brochures, leaflets, sales catalogues
- *Exhibitions*, trade shows and demonstrations
- *Sales promotions* of one kind or another — special offers, free samples, competitions
- *Point-of-sales* displays and merchandising
- *'Free' advertising* through good public relations

It is equally important to organise things so that anyone who wishes to buy your product can do so easily — an effective *distribution* system is essential. Different kinds of products are of course distributed in quite different ways. You would not go to your local supermarket if you wanted to buy some arc-welding equipment; nor would you go to a builder's merchant if you needed a packet of butter and a couple of cartons of milk. Services require yet another type of distribution mechanism, largely due to the fact that they cannot be produced in advance and held in stock until the moment of purchase. For many products and services, some kind of *after-sales service* facilities are also required.

Finally, effective marketing does not just happen by accident. All of the above elements need to be linked together in a meaningful and co-ordinated *marketing plan* which sets out where your company is going and how it proposes to get there.

Over the years academics (and others) have devised many complicated definitions of marketing. There is still no general agreement on a single statement which satisfactorily includes every aspect. Managers of small businesses have neither the time nor the inclination to plough through the naunces of the various alternative definitions available, but really there is no need for them to do so. A very simple definition is perfectly adequate for their requirements:

MARKETING IS SELLING PLUS.

Selling plus what? Selling, plus those other activities listed above which together make the task of selling so much easier to undertake successfully. If you are running a small business, effective marketing on a day-to-day basis involves:

- Doing market research to find out what your customers want.
- Offering them products or services which meet their needs as far as possible.
- Deciding on the appropriate price to charge.
- Ensuring that every potential customer knows that you exist.
- Presenting your firm and the products/services it provides as attractively as possible.
- Setting up a system to make sure that your product or service is easily available to anyone who wants to buy it.
- Providing an appropriate level of after-sales service.
- Convincing customers to give you their business.

SOME MARKETING MISTAKES

Some people seem to have some very strange ideas indeed about what is involved in marketing and what it can do for their company. It is worth taking a few minutes to knock the worst of these marketing myths firmly on the head.

One of the most common is the belief that, somehow or other, marketing is magic — a miracle cure for the company in difficulties. Such managers tends to mutter into their beer: 'What I need is a bit of marketing' — as if it were some kind of wonderful, magical sauce that you can pour over the company, and everything will suddenly be all right. Unfortunately the recipe has not yet been invented. Or, to be more precise, the recipe has been invented, but it is not quite as simple as that. Effective marketing requires a great deal of preliminary thought, careful planning and attention to detail in the implementation phase.

MARKETING IS NOT MAGIC.

It is equally wrong to allow yourself to be overwhelmed by the supposed complexities of what is involved, thus making the second common mistake — that marketing is simply too difficult for the small firm to bother about. Being good at marketing is certainly not easy, but it is by no means impossibly difficult or beyond the reach of the average manager in a small firm. If you are intelligent enough to set up a production line and an accounting system, there is no reason why you should not be equally efficient in your marketing. Much of it is in fact simply sound common sense applied within a structured framework. Part of the problem, of course, is the marketing jargon you hear from self-appointed 'experts'. One owner-manager of a small engineering firm coming out of a high-powered strategic marketing seminar was heard to remark:

> 'I've been doing 80 per cent of that for years—it's just that I never knew what to call it until now!'

He was probably right—and hopefully he derived some additional benefit from the 20 per cent he didn't know.

MARKETING IS NOT IMPOSSIBLY DIFFICULT.

Another common error is the widely-held view that marketing is dreadfully expensive. It is therefore, so the argument goes, only for large and well-established companies, and not really feasible for the small business. There is no doubt that many big firms spend huge amounts of money on marketing. The launch of a new consumer product involving a nationwide television advertising campaign, with associated press advertising, glossy promotional material, trade receptions and so on will cost several million pounds. The fact that you are probably not in a position to engage in that kind of marketing is not a valid argument for doing no marketing at all. If you need a new car, it is a bit stupid to refuse to buy one on the grounds that you can't afford a Rolls-Royce. Almost certainly you will not need to spend this kind of money on marketing at this stage of your company's development, even if you were in a position to do so, which is unlikely. Nevertheless you can be very effective at marketing on a fairly limited budget.

MARKETING NEED NOT BE IMPOSSIBLY EXPENSIVE.

A word of warning is essential at this point. Do not under-resource your marketing effort! Remember that expenditure on marketing is just as much of an investment in the future prosperity of your company as buying a new machine or acquiring larger premises. Unfortunately, many managers in small firms do not see it that way. They regard money spent on marketing as an unnecessary and avoidable outlay. In effect, they relegate to the bottom of their list of corporate priorities the vitally-important task of finding and retaining customers. Do not forget:

MARKETING IS AN INVESTMENT.

A major part of the problem is that, with most other kinds of investment, you can calculate fairly easily and accurately the returns you may reasonably expect. Marketing is not like that. A given sum of money spent wisely can yield a substantial return in terms of increased sales; the same sum spent foolishly can go straight down the drain. The difference between the two is often very difficult to quantify precisely. It will depend on such things as the design of your product and its packaging, the quality and impact of your publicity material, the wording of your mail-shots, perhaps even your own effectiveness as a sales person. Imagination, flair, creativity and innovation are vitally important to marketing success — presenting what you have to offer in an attractive and interesting way to give you an advantage over the competition. If you do not possess these qualities yourself, you must buy them in exactly the same way that you buy legal, financial or technical advice.

Some people unfortunately make the mistake of assuming that the ability to beat the big drum in public is all that is required. The caricature of the marketing manager is of a fast-talking, loudly-dressed, gin-swilling extrovert with an endless supply of doubtful stories. Like all caricatures, there is an element of truth deep down there somewhere. It is perhaps better described by the more balanced observation that if you can't sell yourself, you are unlikely to be able to sell anything else. But here again you must guard against going overboard.

MARKETING IS NOT SIMPLY HOT AIR.

It is important for you to realise that effective marketing also requires the backroom, low-visibility skills of detailed analysis, careful planning, efficient implementation and effective control.

Possibly the most serious marketing mistake of all is to think that it is not really relevant to your particular operation. Hopefully this introductory chapter has convinced you otherwise. In subsequent chapters we will look in greater detail at what is involved in carrying out the various activities involved in good marketing on a day-to-day basis at the level of the individual small firm with limited resources, both human and financial.

Summary of Key Points
1. Marketing is both a philosophy of business and a specific set of business activities.
2. For the small business, marketing may be defined as 'selling plus'— selling, plus certain other activities which will make the task of selling easier.
3. These activities include market research, new product development, pricing, advertising and sales promotion, distribution and the preparation of a marketing plan.
4. Marketing is not a magic cure for a company in difficulties; it requires the investment of time and resources.
5. Effective marketing is not impossibly difficult and need not be incredibly expensive. Imagination and creative flair are required to make a real impact, but detailed analysis, careful planning and effective implementation are also needed.
6. Marketing is not an optional extra — it is a vital necessity for any small firm.

THE ACTIVITIES INVOLVED IN MARKETING

MARKET RESEARCH

PRODUCT DEVELOPMENT

PRICING

ADVERTISING

SALES PROMOTION

PUBLIC RELATIONS

SELLING

DISTRIBUTION

AFTER-SALES SERVICE

PLANNING AND CONTROL

Figure 1. Marketing = Selling +

Case Study: Company A
This enterprise was founded in 1978 by two brothers who for some time had been producing vegetables on a limited scale on their small farm and selling them directly to a highly localised market. Their first move towards processing was simply to wash and pre-pack their produce. However they noticed that there had developed a substantial demand for chilled salads (e.g. coleslaw) as a result of changes in lifestyle and eating habits. Consumers were becoming increasingly health-conscious and more aware of non-traditional foods; housewives were also attracted by the convenience aspect of these products. Moreover demand was growing rapidly (it has been estimated subsequently that at that time the market was growing at just under 20 per cent a year) and local retailers were experiencing considerable difficulties in obtaining good-quality produce on a guaranteed regular basis.

The two brothers therefore embarked on an intensive period of in-house product development based largely on experimentation with alternative recipes and production techniques, assisted by food science expertise bought in on an *ad hoc* basis from one of the local universities. Initially a limited range of unbranded products was sold in bulk to a few local supermarkets; total turnover in 1979 was less than £100,000. Very soon thereafter, the company was supplying most of the major multiples operating in Ireland with 'own label' packs; this business still makes a significant contribution to total sales. In 1985 the company launched its own branded range in Ireland, and by 1987 turnover exceeded £4 million.

Over the past ten years, approximately £2 million has been invested in plant and equipment, including £1m recently spent on a 25,000 square feet extension with a specialised packaging unit capable of extending the shelf life of fresh vegetable products up to fourteen days. This facility has enabled the company to commence exporting to mainland Britain, which it is now doing very successfully indeed. The company estimates that it now holds a 35 per cent share of the Irish market for chilled salad-type products. A total of seventy-five employees is directly involved in the business. In addition, approximately forty local growers are under contract to supply raw produce. The company provides the growers with precise specifications of their requirements, including not only quantities but also varieties and cultural techniques.

2.
Defining Your Market

Marketing is about how you and your company react to the needs of customers and the activities of competitors in the marketplace. But you need to be absolutely clear in your mind about what you mean when you think about 'the market', 'the customer' and 'the competition'. The reason why this is so important is that the answer to virtually any marketing problem you are likely to encounter will be found by going back to your basic analysis of these key elements.

THE MARKET
The market for anything may be defined as all those individuals and organisations currently purchasing a version of the particular product or service in question, or who may do so in the foreseeable future. It is always a very enlightening exercise to sit down with a blank sheet of paper and draw up a list of everybody you can think of who might conceivably buy whatever it is you have to sell. This is useful for two reasons.

- Many small firms make the mistake of defining their market too narrowly. As a result, they sometimes overlook a whole group of valuable potential customers.
- It helps to clarify your thinking by enabling you to define the total extent of your potential market, and to identify the various sub-groups within it.

Take the humble chicken and ham pie as a very simple example. The potential purchasers of that particular product include:

- housewives buying for their family
- people living on their own (e.g. students)
- restaurants, cafés and fast-food outlets
- pubs and clubs
- hotels and guest houses
- industrial caterers
- institutional caterers (e.g. hospitals and schools)

No doubt it will already have occurred to you that there is also a geographical dimension to the chicken and ham pie market. All of these different types of customers may be found:

- in the immediate vicinity of the chicken and ham pie factory
- within the region in which it is located
- in other regions within Ireland
- elsewhere in Europe
- in many other parts of the world.

Thus the total market for chicken and ham pies can be sub-divided in at least two ways:

- by customer type
- by the geographical location of customers

Market segmentation

This process of sub-dividing a market into smaller sub-groups is called *market segmentation*. The principle is very simple to grasp. You can think of the orange you had for breakfast as a total entity, complete with skin — or you can think of it after it has been peeled and separated into a number of segments ready to eat. Either way, it is still an orange! You can think of a market in exactly the same way — either in total, or broken down into its component parts. Where the analogy breaks down, of course, is that all the segments of an orange are more or less the same. But this is not true in the case of a market. Each segment is radically different from all the others.

Figure 2. Market Segmentation

You can think of the market as a whole:

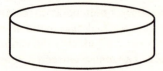

Or divide it into more digestible slices:

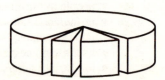

CONSUMER MARKETS

There are many different ways of segmenting a consumer market, i.e. of classifying customers into smaller groups for marketing purposes. You only need to walk around your local shopping centre to see that there is an enormously wide variation in the individuals who together comprise the consumer market. They could be grouped together in terms of their:

- Age/sex/marital status/family size
- Income/occupation/social class
- Area of residence/ geographical location
- Lifestyle
- Social/psychological needs and aspirations
- Usage rate/brand loyalty

Most of these terms are self-explanatory, but some of them may need a little further clarification. Marketing professionals have devised standard definitions of social class based on the income and occupation of the head of the household (see Figure 3) which they use as a convenient form of shorthand. Thus you might hear someone in an advertising agency say something like this:

> 'Our primary target market is ABC_1, married women in the 25-45 age group with two or more children of school age, and living in the Greater Dublin area.'

That statement provides a very clear and concise summary of a specific market segment. When advertisers refer to 'the top end of the market', they mean people classified as AB or ABC_1. The 'bottom end of the market' usually means people in the C_2DE socio-economic groups. The problem with these relatively simple demographic ways of segmenting markets is the assumption that people who have the same superficial personal characteristics (e.g. age, sex and social class) will have the same needs, tastes and buying habits. Experience has shown that, while this may be true for many basic products, there are many others for which this assumption is invalid. For that reason, market researchers have come up with alternative 'segmentation variables'. One such alternative is based on the type of neighbourhood in which people live, defined essentially in terms of the quality of the housing. It is usually referred to as the ACORN system (A Classification Of Residential Neighbourhoods — got it?) Lifestyle is an attempt to sub-divide consumers into broad categories according to their attitudes and behaviour in terms of such things as recreation and entertainment, social issues, political views and so on. The purchasing of many consumers is strongly influenced by social and psychological factors — for example, a housewife determined to keep ahead of (or at least on a par with) a social rival, or a teenager adopting a pop star as a role model. Then again, in some markets it is useful to identify occasional, light, medium and heavy users of the product in question; or those who tend to purchase a particular brand whenever possible (i.e. have a strong brand loyalty). These more complicated psychological ways of segmenting markets are best left to the professionals. The average small business manager would be better advised to stick to the simpler methods, at least initially.

Figure 3. Standard definitions of social/economic class

Class	Occupation of head of household
A/B	Professional and managerial
C_1	Clerical and supervisory
C_2	Skilled manual workers
D	Unskilled manual workers
E	Unemployed, state pensions etc.

INDUSTRIAL MARKETS

The principles of market segmentation can also be applied in markets where the customers are primarily other companies as opposed to individual consumers. In this situation, however, the factors used to sub-divide the total market need to be different, and may include:

- industrial sector
- firm size
- potential volume purchased
- geographical location.

Thus, for example, a particular piece of machinery could be suitable for firms engaged in textiles, furniture, light engineering and transport. So it might be useful to further sub-divide each sector into large, medium and small firms. The market for a component could be segmented in terms of high volume/steady demand, low volume/steady demand, and occasional purchasers.

THE PURPOSE OF MARKET SEGMENTATION

You may now by asking yourself: what is the point of all this market segmentation business? The answer is that *each different segment of the market needs to be treated differently, and may require a different version of the product offered at a different price and sold in a different way.* You need to understand thoroughly the market in which you are

Defining Your Market

operating so that you can devise a marketing strategy that will ensure the long-term survival and profitability of your business. Market segmentation is a useful tool to help you to do so, because the decision about which segments of the market you are going to compete in is crucial to your overall strategy. You have three broad alternatives from which to choose.

- You can try to meet the needs of the market as a whole.
- You can make a deliberate decision to target your efforts on only one or two of the segments you have identified within the total market.
- You can concentrate on a small and specialised niche within the market which has been overlooked or is being ignored by your competitors.

There are advantages and disadvantages associated with each of these strategic alternatives which are discussed in more detail in Chapter 11 (Developing a Marketing Strategy). For the moment, the market for cars is quite a good example we can all relate to. Companies like Ford and Fiat pursue a strategy of servicing the total market, and they do so by treating each segment differently. They have segmented the total market in a very sophisticated way and offer a wide range of models of different sizes and specifications aimed at different segments; these variations are of course reflected in the price. The advertising and promotional methods they use to sell fleets of cars to large companies are quite different from how they go about selling to the general public. Other manufacturers such as Jaguar, Porsche and Rolls-Royce focus their efforts on catering for the needs of a specialised segment of the total market by producing only high performance luxury sports cars, or super-luxury prestige cars. Smaller firms which specialise in restoring or making modern reproductions of classic vintage cars are examples of niche marketing in the automobile industry. Like the car-makers, you need to do a number of things.

- Examine your market closely.
- Segment it.
- Choose those segments in which you wish to compete.
- Profile your marketing effort accordingly.

THE CUSTOMER

The concept of 'the customer' is so fundamental to business that you are probably wondering why it is necessary to spend any time at all sorting out what it means. The reason is that it is possible to identify at least three distinctly different types of customers:

- *The end-user* of your product or service who purchases it for his or her own personal use, or for a member of his/her family;
- *The intermediate customer* who buys it from you in order to re-sell it to someone else;
- *The professional purchasing officer* who is employed by a large company or a government department to buy things used by other employees of the organisation.

The intermediate customer

The end-users are, of course, the general public, often housewives. If you are a manufacturer of consumer goods, the intermediate customer is likely to be a supermarket buyer, or a wholesaler, or perhaps an agent/distributor. If you manufacture engineering or electronic components, for example, there may well be no intermediaries involved. The product is sold directly to the buyer, quite often on a sub-contract basis. However companies of this kind can have intermediate customers — specialist suppliers of a wide range of assorted bits and pieces. Firms in the services sector may also have to deal with both intermediate customers and end-users. For example, an industrial caterer will have to satisfy the requirements of the large firm or government department which has contracted for the supply of the service and also meet the needs of the individuals who consume the meals provided on a daily basis.

This last point needs to be emphasised. You need to find out as much as you can about both types of customer; it is not a case of one or the other. You have to satisfy the needs of both groups if you are to hold on to their business. To do this effectively for each of these different types of customer, you need to know more than simply what they buy. You also need to know how and why they buy.

How people buy

There are substantial differences in the way different types of customers set about the task of buying something. As far as individual consumers are concerned, the notion that they often buy things on the spur of the moment does not square with the facts. Impulse buying can happen, but it is actually quite rare. The more typical scenario is that, before a purchase is made, consumers acquire a lot of information about the various alternatives available, and evaluate them by comparing price, quality and so on. They will be influenced in this process by the type of information they are presented with in advertising and publicity material, perhaps by examining, sampling or testing the product, by talking to their friends, and by their own previous experience in buying similar goods or services in the past. You can see this kind of pre-purchase activity very clearly simply by thinking about your own behaviour before you buy, say, a new car. As a rough rule, the more expensive the item to be purchased, the greater will be the time and effort consumers devote to finding out about and choosing between alternatives. People do not worry too much about buying a box of matches, but they do give a great deal of thought to whether or not they are making the right choice when they buy a new kitchen or a new carpet.

Moreover, their reasons for choosing one particular version of a product or service rather than another are much more complex than a straightforward comparison of relative prices. In a sense, when you buy anything you are making a statement to the rest of the world about the sort of person you are, or the sort of person you would like people to think you are — what other people think is quite important to most of us. In other words, consumers are also influenced by the prestige or status derived from buying one thing rather than another, and by how that purchase will contribute to the overall image of themselves they are trying to project to the world at large. A housewife making choices in a supermarket may well be strongly influenced by her views on what constitutes a healthy diet, or on how she might help to protect the environment. To discover the reasons why people buy things, you often need to pay attention to their motives and attitudes as well as to their more obvious physical needs.

Professional buyers

Professional buyers approach the task in quite a different way. Their primary motive is to obtain the best possible deal, with the ultimate objective of maximising profits or efficiency by keeping costs to an absolute minimum. But it is a major mistake to assume that price is the only relevant factor for professional buyers. Their purchasing decisions are influenced by things such a reliability, availability, delivery, the need to have a guaranteed source of supply, as well as the more obvious requirement that whatever you are selling them will do the job for which it was intended. Not only do they have different motives from consumers; professional buyers carry out the task of buying in a totally different way.

If you are in the sort of business which sells to the supermarket chains, you will soon run up against the 'list' system. There are marginal differences between the multiples. Some of them operate through centralised national or regional buying points, while others allow the manager of an individual outlet a considerable degree of freedom. But in general, buyers are only permitted to buy from companies which appear on the list of recognised suppliers approved by their head office. If you are not 'listed', you have no chance; being 'de-listed' is one of the worst things that can happen to you. This system often presents the small firm with a major dilemma. It is almost a 'Catch 22' situation. Major buyers would say: 'You cannot become one of our suppliers unless you are listed, and you cannot be listed until you have proved your reliability and the quality of your products by supplying us to our satisfaction for a reasonable length of time.' The only way out of this dilemma is to keep pushing, politely, until you are given a trial order — and then pull out all the stops to make absolutely certain that nothing goes wrong while you are fulfilling it.

Many government departments, local authorities, semi-state agencies and big companies use the competitive tender system for much of their buying. Here again, you will quite often encounter the list of approved suppliers from whom tenders will be accepted. If you sell to this type of customer, it is essential to make sure that you are 'listed'. This is usually not too difficult to arrange, but may well involve an inspection of your premises and a check that you are a bona fide company.

There is one other aspect of how these big organisations buy which you should be aware of. The person who actually writes out the order is often not the most important individual involved in the purchasing decision. In the case of large or technically complex orders, the final decision is usually taken by a group of people (e.g. a Board of Directors, or a Hospital Management Committee) rather than by a single person. The members of this group will arrive at a decision based on the advice they have received from other people in the organisation — technical experts, accountants and so on. Sometimes this process of consultation takes quite a long time to complete before a final choice is made. The advice given to the decision-makers is obviously of crucial importance in determining which supplier is given the order. You can improve your chances significantly by identifying and influencing the key figures involved in this complex buying process.

THE COMPETITION

One thing you can be absolutely certain about in an uncertain world is that you will encounter competition. Even if you are fortunate enough to develop a completely new and totally unique product, you can rest assured that somebody, somewhere, will soon come up with an alternative version of it, quite possibly cheaper and/or better than yours.

Competition is inevitable, so it is essential that you pay attention to identifying your actual and potential competitors.

Everything is competition

In one sense, everything else your customers might spend their money on is a competitor. If for any reason they have less to spend, then the competition for a share of a smaller cake will become much more intense for all concerned — including you. That is why you need to keep an eye on what is happening in the broader business environment — unemployment, inflation, interest rates and so on. You must also make sure that you take a broad enough view of your more immediate competitors. It is a mistake to focus your attention too narrowly. As a result of doing so, you might overlook a major potential threat looming up over the distant horizon. If you are in the business of marketing soft drinks and 'mixers', your obvious immediate competitors are the other firms in your area which offer a broadly similar product range. But you are also in competition with a very wide range of other beverages. Who would have imagined twenty years ago that bottled spring water would take such a large share of this traditional and long-established market?

Another example of competition is provided by a small firm in England which was doing very well supplying those little round tins in which pipe tobacco used to be sold. Someone not involved in the 'tobacco tin' business at all suggested to the big tobacco companies that a plastic pouch would be a much more cost-effective form of packaging for this particular product. Subsequent market research demonstrated that the great majority of pipe smokers actually preferred the plastic pouch. The outcome was that the supplier of tins soon found himself in serious difficulties as his customers switched over to the alternative product he could not provide. The point of the story is that he thought he was in the business of supplying tins; he was in fact competing in a much broader market which could be defined as the market for airtight and moisture-proof packaging materials.

Your immediate competition

You need to take a similarly broad view of the market you are serving, and watch out for competition from less obvious sources which might be a threat to you in the longer term. As an absolute minimum, you need to identify your direct and immediate competitors and make an effort to find out:

- how many of them there are
- which of them are the most important
- what are their strengths and weaknesses

Here again a useful starting point is to take a blank sheet of paper and simply draw up a list of your competitors in order of importance, with a comment against each one. When you have done this, the overall structure of the market in which you are operating will become fairly clear. You will soon find that you are faced with one of the following competitive situations:

- a market served by a large number of relatively small firms, all offering more or less the same thing;
- a market in which a few large firms share the bulk of the business between them, with a number of smaller firms fighting it out for what is left;
- a market dominated by a single very large supplier in which smaller firms can survive only by keeping a low profile and/or concentrating on a very small part of the total market.

It is important to analyse your competitors in this way. This will provide you with some valuable guidelines when you start to develop your marketing strategy. Before you begin to do that, however, you need to find out a lot more about your customers, your competitors and the business environment within which you must operate.

In other words, you need to do some market research.

Summary of Key Points
1. The market for anything includes everyone who currently buys this product or service, or who may do so in the foreseeable future. Many small firms define their market too narrowly.
2. Markets can be sub-divided in various ways. These sub-divisions are usually referred to as 'segments' of the market. Identifying the different segments within a market will enable you to focus your marketing activities better, because different segments may need to be treated differently.
3. You need to decide whether to try and cater for the market as a whole, or to target your efforts on only one or two segments of it, or to concentrate even more narrowly on a small and specialised niche.
4. Many businesses have two different types of customers—the final consumer or 'end-user' who buys a product or service for his of her own personal use, and the intermediate customer who buys it in order to re-sell it to someone else. To be successful, you need to identify and satisfy the needs of both types of customer.
5. For some small firms, 'the customer' is a professional purchasing

officer employed by a government department or some other large organisation.
6. It is a major mistake to assume that people buy things solely on the basis of price. Their purchasing decisions are influenced by many other factors. You need to find out as much as you can about why people buy things. This will involve paying attention to their motives and attitudes as well as their more obvious physical needs.
7. Competition is inevitable and unavoidable. You must identify your actual and potential competitors, find out as much as you can about them, and keep an eye of their activities.

Case Study: Company B
This enterprise was founded in 1976 by three former employees of a large distributor of food products in Northern Ireland. At that time, many of the major manufacturers of branded consumer goods were in the process of implementing a major change in their distribution strategy, in that they were actively seeking to reduce their costs by closing provincial storage and distribution depots and by reducing their sales forces. This they achieved by sub-contracting these roles to locally-based agencies. In the specific case of Northern Ireland, the continuing civil unrest there merely served to increase the reluctance of many manufacturers to maintain a direct presence.

The founders of Company B became aware that their original employer had turned down an approach from Colgate-Palmolive on the grounds that the suggested product range was incompatible with their own well-established sphere of activity. They bid for and obtained a contract to distribute Colgate-Palmolive products in the Province. Their initial start-up capital was £25; they rented a warehouse and purchased a lorry on HP. In their first year of trading, they distributed £45,000 worth of products on a rate per ton basis and made 'either a profit or a loss' of £5. They were then appointed sales agents, and by 1979 their turnover had increased to £750,000. Over the next few years, the company widened its product portfolio considerably and rapidly moved back into the food industry. In 1982, it took over a major competitor in Northern Ireland and subsequently widened the scope of its activities by establishing sales offices and distribution depots in the south of England and in Dublin. The company has also diversified into manufacturing and now markets under its own brand a range of meat and chicken pies, creamed rice and other desserts, and butter. In effect, it has developed from being a small-scale importer to Northern Ireland to a relatively large-scale exporter, not only of its own products but also those of other NI food manufacturers and processors. In response to the classic marketing question 'what business are you really in?', its managing director defines it now as essentially a 'food broker', looking after the interests of large companies in a small market (i.e. Northern Ireland), and of small companies in a large market (i.e. Great Britain).

The situation at present is that, in addition to its own manufacturing activities, the company distributes goods on behalf of more than twenty other manufacturers, has an annual turnover of around £26 million, and directly employs 120 people.

3.
Doing Market Research

Imagine trying to drive home late at night with no lights and with both eyes firmly shut. It is a fairly safe bet that anybody crazy enough to attempt such a thing would end up either in hospital or in the mortuary. Trying to run a business without ever doing any market research falls into exactly the same category—a form of behaviour which no one in their right mind would seriously consider. Yet that is precisely how many small business managers behave. They will tell you that they 'rely on experience', or that they have a 'gut feeling' for how the market is going to go. There is no doubt that somebody who has been in a particular line of business for a long time does, in fact, develop a 'feel' for trends in the market. This can, of course, be very useful indeed for planning purposes. But quite often this depth of expertise is simply not there. Even worse, some managers successfully kid themselves that they have nothing more to learn. In other words, the success they have had to date is due more to luck than judgment. Others will concede that market research is 'a good thing' in principle, but they are firmly convinced that it is both very difficult and very expensive and therefore something which only big firms can really hope to do effectively.

Nothing could be further from the truth. Have you ever looked at a competitor's product and compared it with your own? How is it packaged? How much does it cost? How does it measure up in terms of quality? Have you ever seen something on television or read about it in a magazine and reflected on how this might affect your own business — a change in the mortgage rate, a new manufacturing process, a feature on the changing tastes and habits of the affluent, middle-class suburban housewife? Have you ever sat down and thought long and hard about why you lost a particular order? If you have asked yourself any of these questions, then you have already done some market research!

MARKET RESEARCH IS COLLECTING AND USING INFORMATION WHICH IS USEFUL IN PLANNING YOUR COMPANY'S MARKETING ACTIVITIES.

In common with all simple definitions, this one raises nearly as many questions as it answers, including:
- What kind of information?
- How can it be collected?
- How should it be used?

WHAT KIND OF INFORMATION?

To run your business effectively, you need to know as much as possible about four key aspects of the constantly-changing world in which you must operate:
- Your customers
- Your competitors
- Your own performance
- The overall business environment

Customers

The precise details of the information you need will vary according to the type of business you are running, but some basic data is essential for virtually any type of business. This absolute minimum of customer information includes:
- Who is likely to buy this product/service?
- What are they buying at present?
- What factors affect their choice?
- Where, when and how do they buy?

The typical answer of many managers in smaller firms to the first of these questions is 'anybody'! A few minutes' reflection is usually sufficient to convince them otherwise. If you are still not convinced, go out and ask a passing bricklayer how often he buys ladies' tights. You need to build up a detailed and accurate profile of your potential customers, dividing them up into broadly similar sub-groups as appropriate. In consumer markets, the sort of information you will find useful for describing your customers includes very basic things like their:
- age, sex and marital status
- income/occupation/social class
- area of residence

In industrial markets, it is useful to group customers on the basis of things like their:
- type of industry
- size
- location

You also need to know roughly how many potential customers there are out there, and to have some idea about whether the total number of customers is likely to increase, decrease or remain more or less stable over the next five years or so. At this stage of your development, you are unlikely to need to spend a great deal of time and effort developing an accurate estimate of the size of the total national market — what good would it do you? As far as you are concerned, the basic problem is quite simply to make sure that there are enough potential customers around for you to make a decent living. If you are experiencing some difficulty in identifying potential customers, the best advice you can be given is to think hard and long before you go any further. If there is no market, or if the market is not big enough, there is no way that you can hope to survive for very long. Forget it, and try something else!

When you are looking at what your potential customers are currently buying, it is also useful to try and find out roughly how much they buy over a given period, say, a year, and how frequently they make a purchase. It can be helpful to discover whether they tend to purchase the same brand or version of a product all the time, or whether they switch about from one brand to another without bothering too much — this is called their 'brand loyalty' in marketing jargon.

Non-price factors

The reason why people choose one supplier rather than another is possibly the most useful piece of information you could find out about your customers. It is also possibly the most difficult to obtain, because the answer will depend on psychological factors which the customers themselves may not even be aware of. Their choice could be dictated simply by convenience or habit, but it could equally well be due to deep-seated motives and attitudes. Thus, their purchasing behaviour is influenced by their need to:

- imitate someone they look up to
- impress somebody (or everybody)
- enhance their own self-image.

Non-price factors of this kind are usually expressed in terms of how people respond to the different designs, styles, presentations, advertising and promotions they are offered by alternative suppliers. Their behaviour will also be influenced by their previous experience of buying and using a particular product or service, and this in turn will strongly influence their loyalty to it. This point is easily understood if you apply it to your own situation. If you have taken your children out on a Saturday afternoon, they will usually demand to be fed at some stage of the proceedings. You might take them to a fast-food outlet which turns out to be anything but fast, where the staff are at best surly and possibly even downright rude to you, and where the hamburgers and chips are greasy and under-cooked. The likely outcome is that you will be a less-than-satisfied customer. Quite possibly you will also be up half the night tending to the needs of your offspring, who are taking it in turns to be violently ill! The result of a negative experience of this kind is that you will be most unlikely to go back to that particular establishment. On the other hand, if everything has gone according to plan without any problems, it is likely that you will be quite happy to go back again for a repeat visit. In other words, if the customer's experience in using a product or service has been positive, they are more likely to repeat that pattern of behaviour again in the future.

Non-price factors also affect the purchasing behaviour of companies and other organisations. It is not suggested that price is totally irrelevant. But in the fairly common situation where a number of suppliers are quoting more or less the same price, then factors such as technical performance, proven reliability, delivery, after-sales service and so on become very important indeed. It is very useful to know which of these factors are important to your potential customers because this will help you to do an effective selling job. You would, for example, have some guidelines on what features and benefits you should emphasise in your publicity material, as well as when you are talking to clients.

The buying process

You also need to give some thought to the actual process of buying. What do customers do between the time that they decide to buy something and the point at which they make the purchase? How do they go about placing an order? A housewife who has decided to buy a new item of furniture will probably visit most of the furniture showrooms in the area where she lives in order to discover what is currently on offer, comparing and contrasting the various alternatives available. Having narrowed the field, she will eventually make the decisive trip, possibly with her husband in tow, to make the final choice and place her order. A large firm intending to buy a new piece of machinery may well invite quotations from several different suppliers. These are then compared, and a number of machines may be installed on a trial basis in order to monitor their performance in detail. The decision on which one to buy is often made by a committee of some kind (perhaps even by the Board of Directors), whose members will consider reports on performance during trial, specification, financing arrangements and so on. It often happens that the person who actually places the order is relatively junior, and does not really have a significant role in the purchasing decision. A government department will usually draw up a detailed specification for whatever it wants to buy and then invite approved suppliers to submit tenders. Taking the trouble to tease out in some detail the way in which your customers set about the task of buying can be very helpful in making some of your subsequent marketing decisions — for example, your choice of the most appropriate distribution system.

Competitors
You are putting yourself at a severe disadvantage if you do not make an effort to find out as much as you can about your competitors. The sort of information you need includes:
- How many of them are there?
- How do you compare with them?
- What are their strengths and weaknesses?

As an absolute minimum, you should identify who your competitors are — if you believe you don't have any competitors, think again! You are almost certainly kidding yourself. It is also helpful to try and identify the relative importance of each of your competitors in terms of their share of the total market, but you should not waste too much time trying to be absolutely accurate on this point. For your purposes, it is enough to know that Company A is the major threat, and that it probably accounts for about 40 per cent of total sales in your area. The fact that it has an audited market share of 36.4 per cent nationally is not really all that relevant to you.

It is much more important from your point of view to assess how you measure up in comparison with your main competitors. To do this, you need to collect as much information as you can about their activities, including:
- What products/services do they provide?
- How much do they charge?
- What kind of distribution system do they have?
- Do they advertise? If so, where? What key points do they emphasise?
- Do they have a brochure or a sales catalogue? If so, try to get hold of it.
- How do they do their selling?
- Do they provide any kind of after-sales service?
- Do they have a good reputation?

When you have this basic information, you need to make some sense out of it. One very simple way of doing this is to take a large blank sheet of paper and write down the left hand side a list of the key aspects of their marketing activity — product range, price and so on. Then write the names of your competitors across the top. By drawing an appropriate few lines, you will have a series of boxes — now fill in the empty boxes as best you can! Once you have done this you should be in a much better position to make a realistic and comprehensive assessment of your competitors' strengths and weaknesses, and your own. This will give you some valuable guidelines on how you should plan your own future activities. Incidentally, it is absolutely vital that you try to be as objective as possible when you are doing this. It is pure folly to kid yourself that things are better (or worse) than they actually are.

Figure 4. Market research is collecting and using information

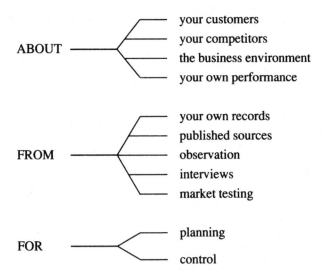

Your own performance

You might be surprised to find this appearing under the heading of market research. After all, you may already have a comprehensive accounting and costing system which monitors your firm's performance over a wide range of activities. If you are in manufacturing or processing, you probably also have some kind of quality control system to ensure that your output is up to the standard you require. But these are

internal performance indicators; you also need to monitor your performance externally. This will involve trying to find out:
- Whether potential customers are aware that you exist; and
- If they are, what they think of you.

This raises some fundamental questions about the effectiveness of your advertising and publicity. A basic requirement for the success of any business is that every potential customer should be aware of your existence, and of what you have to offer. Can you claim with hand on heart that you have met this requirement? Are you quite certain that the message you want to communicate is getting through to the right people? All of them? If you do not know whether it is or not, it is worth your while to find out. Even if you can satisfy yourself that the great majority of your potential customers have at least heard of you, there then arises a supplementary question — what do they think of you? Does your company have a good or a bad reputation in terms of things like product quality, delivery dates, reliability, honesty/integrity/straight dealing? In other words, what is your corporate image, and do you need to take positive action to try and change it?

THE BUSINESS ENVIRONMENT

You do not run your business in a vacuum. The environment in which you operate is changing all the time for all kinds of reasons. You need to be aware of what is happening in the world at large because some of these changes may present you with valuable new opportunities, or alternatively threaten your future profitability, and perhaps even your long-term survival. A useful way of sorting out the details of this enormously wide range of possible influences on your firm is to consider them under four separate headings:
- Economic
- Technological
- Social
- Political and legal

The economy

Economic factors are totally outside your control, but they can have a profound influence on the demand for your product or service. At the most basic level, Ireland is the only country in Europe in which the population is still increasing, and is projected to continue rising until well into the next century. This implies that the demand for goods and services of all kinds is also likely to increase, provided that we can maintain the current average level of prosperity, simply because there will be more consumers around. Changes in the age structure of the population will be reflected in the changing pattern of demand for various goods and services. One of the big issues, of course, is whether we can at least maintain the current standard of living into the 1990s and beyond. Unemployment is high, and likely to remain so in the foreseeable future. This tends to depress the total amount of disposable income available nationwide. But if a new factory is built in your area, the total spending power of the local population will rise. If bank lending rates goes up, mortgage interest payments will also rise, and people in general will have much less to spend. Again, if interest rates rise, money will become very much tighter for businesses of all kinds — so you will find it harder to get them to pay their bills on time, or at all. In a similar way, changes in taxation rates, or in the inflation rate, will affect total demand in one way or another. Fluctuations in the exchange rate are also significant because imported finished goods and raw materials will become more or less expensive, with an obvious knock-on effect in the price of things in the shops. If government expenditure on health and education is increased, that is good news for firms in the construction industry, and for suppliers of a wide range of products and services. These are just a few examples of how economic factors can directly influence an individual firm. It is up to you to identify which of them are most relevant to your own operation.

Technology
Technological change occurs in every industry. It can affect any stage of the production process, including:
- the design, performance and specification of products and services
- manufacturing techniques
- marketing and distribution

Believe it or not, there were some characters around in the early 1900s who spent a lot of time convincing themselves and others that these new-fangled motor cars would never catch on. There are literally thousands of examples of this kind of situation where a new and better way of meeting a basic need arrives on the scene and very rapidly replaces what was there previously. The ball-point pen and felt tips have largely replaced the fountain pen. Digital watches have made substantial inroads into sales of the traditional type of wristwatch. Electrically-driven drills, hedge-clippers and lawnmowers are replacing the older types of tool which relied on muscle-power. Technological advances are also incorporated into the production process — for example, computer-controlled machine tools. Some firms in the textile industry have demonstrated that it is possible to overcome the challenge posed by cheap-labour foreign competitors by making full use of the very latest high-speed equipment. Computerised reservation systems have revolutionised some aspects of the service industries. Marketing and distribution techniques have also benefitted. Radio and television commercials were simply not available to our grandfathers; the portable demonstration video was not available to our fathers. Polystyrene, cling film and the blister pack have transformed the way in which many products are packaged. Bar coding has made it possible for retailers to maintain a much more accurate check on stock levels. The examples are so numerous that it is difficult knowing quite when to stop, but the basic point is very simple. You cannot afford to ignore technological change, and you need to keep up with the latest developments which may affect any aspect of your business.

Social change
It may not be immediately apparent to you, but broad social trends are reflected in the types of goods and services people demand. Their needs and wants change in line with changes in their attitudes, which in turn are influenced by the media and other areas of public discussion and debate. The public attitude to health is quite a good example of this process in action. There is an increasing awareness of high death rates from heart disease, lung cancer and so on, arising largely from the efforts of the medical profession in educating us about various aspects of our traditional lifestyle. This has affected the pattern of demand in all kinds of ways. There has been a movement away from butter to low-cholesterol low-fat spreads; from the traditional fried breakfast of bacon and eggs to high-fibre muesli and orange juice. It is now a positive advantage to display the words 'low fat' or 'sugar free' or 'low salt' on virtually everything from a can of peas to a pre-cooked lasagne. The demand for training shoes, track suits and sports equipment of all kinds is substantially higher than it was ten or fifteen years ago.

Another interesting example of the impact of social change in action is the vast increase in foreign travel dating from the advent of relatively cheap packages tours in the 1960s. As a result, Irish people are now thoroughly familiar with pizzas, pasta, paella and pâté; school meals menus now often include spaghetti bolognese and chicken curry. This relatively recent internationalisation of our eating habits can be clearly seen on the shelves of any supermarket. The consumption of wine has soared, to the detriment of more traditional beverages.

A more recent social trend which is certain to have a major impact on our lifestyle is the growing concern for environmental protection. As with economic and technological change, you need to be aware of broad social trends and to move with the times to accommodate them.

Political/legal factors
In our kind of political system, we the people elect a government, which then proceeds to pass laws, manage the economy, enter into trade and other agreements with foreign countries, and so on. From the point of view of running your business, it is largely irrelevant whether or not you agree with what the government of the day is doing. The relevant point is that its policies can have a direct and immediate impact on your prospects. Take legislation as an example. What do you think happened to the demand for crash helmets when a law was passed requiring that everyone riding a motor-bike had to wear one? On a broader point, joining the Common Market was probably the most important single political decision taken by an Irish government in recent years, and has resulted in a whole new raft of problems and opportunities. Depending on what business you are in, you may well be very interested in the 'Green Pound', or in the European Monetary System, or in new regulations in respect of the Regional Fund and the Social Fund. This process will continue up to and beyond the scheduled completion of the unified internal market in 1992. Here again, you need to be aware of what is happening and how it may affect you.

It is, of course, totally impossible for a single individual who is already carrying a heavy workload to spend a lot of time on the huge task of continuously monitoring the overall business environment. But you do need to try and keep up-to-date by reading technical and trade journals, and through the newspapers and television. You also need to sit down from time to time and reflect on the possible consequences for your business of any actual or predicted changes in the general background which you have picked up on the way.

HOW CAN INFORMATION BE COLLECTED?
Many large companies spend a lot of money commissioning market research from professional agencies which use sophisticated techniques of data collection and analysis. This option is often not available to the smaller firm because of the high costs involved, but you should not dismiss it too quickly. A small-scale study can be surprisingly inexpensive, and grant-aid may be available from a government agency. However, most small businesses have to adopt a DIY approach, at least initially.

Doing Market Research

This need not imply poor work and bad results. There are a number of techniques available which are simple to apply, inexpensive and effective. These include:
- digging out information which already exists
- observation
- doing interviews
- testing the market on a limited scale

Using existing information

It is surprising just how much you can find out about a particular market by searching out information which is already available. The way to go about it is to do the following.
- Decide in advance *exactly* what information you need.
- Think carefully about who might have that information.
- Ask the right questions.
- Don't give up too easily.

The main sources of this type of information are:
- Competitors' sales catalogues and brochures
- Trade journals and trade associations
- Special features in quality newspapers
- Directories of one kind or another
- Government departments and semi-state organisations
- Local and national industrial development agencies
- Banks
- Your own company's internal records

A useful starting point is to get hold of your competitors' promotional material. You can deduce quite a lot about your potential customers by studying it carefully. Who is it aimed at? What points are emphasised to appeal to the customer? What styles and designs are currently available? And so on. You can then begin to develop and refine your knowledge of the market by looking at back issues of the appropriate trade journal; you should also start buying it on a regular basis. If you don't even know the names of the trade journals in your particular field, go along to the reference section of your local public library and ask them to find out for you. The bigger public libraries often have a collection of commercial and business directories which may be useful. Incidentally, don't forget that you have immediate and free access to one of the most useful directories of all — the phone book. If you want to do a mail-shot, say, to every farmer living in the South-East Region, the Golden Pages include a nearly complete listing of all their names and addresses. Similarly, if you want to find out how many suppliers of agricultural tractors there are in the country, you can do so very easily. You will also quite often find there is a trade association for manufacturers and distributors of the particular product or service you are interested in. The permanent officials of these bodies are very knowledgeable indeed about all aspects of their trade and are usually willing to help if you approach them in the right way.

Government departments
Government departments and the various semi-state agencies have at their disposal an incredible amount of data. The problem usually is to get what you want without being snowed under by a mass of statistics which are not all that relevant to your needs. The trick is to learn how to ask the right question. An official in an industrial development agency in Dublin expressed the problem very clearly:

> 'This character phoned me the other day and explained that he runs a small business down the country somewhere. He then asked whether I thought he should try selling his product in the North. How am I expected to answer a question like that? If he had asked me to give him the names of two or three distributors he could talk to — that I can do, no problem.'

All the industrial development agencies have a library containing market reports and studies of various kinds. These are usually referred to by some fancy name such as a 'data bank' or a 'market intelligence centre'. Do not be put off by this — go in there and ask! However it is not usually a good idea to simply turn up on the doorstep without prior warning. You will find it much more productive if you telephone in advance, explain what you are looking for as precisely as you can, and make an appointment to see someone.

The banks
The banks also provide reports and briefings about various topics, but these tend to be fairly general in their approach and are unlikely to provide the detail you require, although they are useful background material. Your local bank manager is unlikely to provide very much direct help with your research — he or she has neither the time nor the expertise to do it for you — but he or she may well be able to suggest the names of people it would be worthwhile contacting.

Your own company records
The records you have to keep in order to run your business efficiently are also a rich source of market information. Every business is differ-

ent, and will have different information needs. It is obviously not really feasible to give detailed guidelines which will cover every possible situation. You will have to do a bit of creative thinking about your own requirements and how they might be met, but the basic point still holds — there is a huge amount of useful data already available, both within your own firm and elsewhere. It is worth the effort involved in digging it out.

Observation

A young food scientist was trying to set up a business manufacturing pre-cooked frozen meals. He wanted to find out what kind of people buy these products, what was the price range of similar products already on the market, how they were packaged and displayed, and so on. Rather than spend a lot of his limited capital on commissioning research, he was advised to accompany his wife on her next shopping trip and to spend some time at the chilled display cabinets in his local supermarket. He was further advised to repeat the exercise several times, going to different shopping centres on different days of the week. The information he obtained in this way was neither as detailed nor as accurate as a professional market research study would have produced — but he obtained maybe 80 per cent of the information he needed at virtually zero cost other than his own time. The point of this true story is that simple observation can be a very useful and cost-effective research technique.

Visiting a trade show or exhibition is another way in which you can learn a great deal simply by keeping your eyes (and ears) open. Quite apart from the obvious need to inspect closely what your competitors have on display, you should collect as much of their publicity material as you can. You might also take ncte of what kind of enquiries are received and how they are handled.

The opportunities for doing research by observation are many and varied. Here again it is up to you to be imaginative in going about it in a way which is relevant to your own information needs.

Interviews

You can also collect information simply by talking to people. The word 'interview' probably conjures up a mental image of a pleasant middle-aged woman equipped with a clip-board and a bright smile, but the term can include anything from a brief telephone call to an hour-long face-to-face open-ended discussion. If you decide to do any interviews, you must take care to ensure that the information you collect is valid and reliable. You must make sure that the people you contact are truly representative of the group you want to find out about, and you should interview enough of them to make sure you are not being misled. You will usually find that a consistent pattern begins to emerge fairly quickly from the answers you are getting, with the same points being repeated more or less continuously. You will find that most people are prepared to talk to you if you approach them politely, and you will be surprised at how much information is forthcoming. You should prepare for your interview well in advance by deciding exactly what information you want to get from them, and then devising a set of questions which will obtain that information. Try and ask 'open' questions which encourage people to talk, rather than 'closed' questions which invite a 'yes' or 'no' answer. You need to be careful to avoid ambiguous or badly-phrased questions (e.g. 'Do you take a bath regularly? — Yes, once a year, every year'). You should try and develop a questionnaire which you can fill in as you go along, or else immediately after the interview is over. This will ensure that you ask everybody the same questions and will make it much easier to make sense of the results. It is also a good idea to try out your questionnaire on a few people and change it if it does not work particularly well.

Problems to avoid

There are some fairly obvious pitfalls to avoid. If you are trying to interview housewives, do not sidle up to them in a dark car-park in the rain — you are unlikely to be well received. Do not interview customers in a supermarket or a shopping centre without first obtaining the permission of the manager. If you are contacting housewives by telephone, pick a time when they are not likely to be preparing a meal or putting the children to bed. If you are researching the market for a consumer product, it is essential that you also talk to the retail buyer as well as to the eventual consumer. Similarly in industrial markets, it is often possible to identify a group of key people who know the scene backwards and can draw on years of experience in a particular area. For example, if you were investigating the market for window frames, it would be useful to talk to architects, quantity surveyors and builders' merchants. When you contact them initially, you should first of all ask if it is a convenient time to talk to them; if not, try to arrange an appointment at a more suitable time. Be open about the fact that you are doing some market research — people do not take kindly to having the wool pulled over their eyes. You will often find that they are quite flattered to be asked their professional opinion and that they will co-operate with you.

But do not be surprised, and do not give up, if the first two or three people you contact tell you to get lost.

Test marketing

It is often possible to introduce a new product or service on a limited scale for a short period of time and in a restricted geographical area in order to see how it goes. If it is not well received, you can drop it and try something else. Or you can do a radical re-think of the whole project without doing major damage to the business as a whole. If sales take off at once fairly well, you may be on to a winner. The more likely outcome is that you will learn some valuable lessons about some aspect of the operation which you will need to revise before proceeding any further. Many large companies do this kind of test marketing on a regular basis.

In some situations, research is needed to establish whether the product does what it is supposed to do, and whether or not it is acceptable to the customer. A new food product is a simple example of what may be required. Quite apart from the need to comply with health, labelling and other statutory regulations, there is the minor detail of finding out if people like it enough to actually buy it. This could be done by setting up a panel of fifteen to twenty housewives who are prepared to test the product with their families and let you know their reactions. You could also ask them some additional questions, like how much they would expect to pay in the shops for this kind of product. What you must not do is to rely entirely on the experience of your own immediate family — a sample of one is always suspect.

COMMISSIONING MARKET RESEARCH

As a broad general rule, you should not rush out and commission a professional market research agency to undertake a particular project unless and until you are certain that you cannot get the information you need in any other way. It might also be worthwhile employing a consultant if:

- You do not have the time or the expertise needed to do a good job on your own.
- You have been specifically asked to provide a development agency or your bank with a full-scale professionally-executed report.
- You are able to obtain a grant or some other kind of financial assistance to do so.

Apart from the obvious advantages of saving your time and bringing to bear a higher level of expertise than you possess, a professional market researcher can often obtain detailed information from sources not normally available to a private individual, providing you with a totally objective view of the problem.

There are three basic steps involved in commissioning market research:
- Finding a consultant
- Briefing the consultant
- Evaluating the consultant's proposal

Finding a consultant

Identifying possible consultants is fairly straightforward. You will find most of them listed in the telephone book. But there are a number of pitfalls you should know about.

First, you should realise that market research agencies are not like accountants, lawyers and doctors, in that there is nothing in law to prevent absolutely anybody putting a plate on the door and going into business as a marketing consultant, even if they know little or nothing about it! There is a professional body to which the established reputable companies belong, but membership of it is voluntary, rather than a statutory requirement for practising in this field. There are unfortunately a few fly-by-night operators around, and you should make sure that you only approach a reputable agency which will do a good job for you. You can easily find out whether a particular consultancy is any good by asking a few people in your local business community. The development agencies keep a register of approved consultants, which is also very useful if you need to find a specialist in a particular area.

Secondly, it is not a good idea to try to have market research professionally done on the cheap. A decent consultant will say to you either:
- Tell me what you want to find out, and I will tell you how much that will cost; or
- Tell me how much you want to spend, and I will tell you what I can provide within that budget.

The alarm bells should start to ring if you find someone promising to supply everything you require for next to nothing. However there are ways to economise. One of the best is to employ a marketing student on a temporary basis — there are plenty of them around. But you should remember that, by definition, a student is still learning the tricks of the trade. It is unreasonable to expect a top-class professional job from a student, although you may be lucky enough to get one if you have the good fortune to find a top-class student.

You should also consider obtaining proposals from more than one agency. But bear in mind that you may be asked to pay the costs of preparing the proposal if you do not proceed to commission the project. There is no single way of carrying out a particular piece of research. Different consultants may well come up with different approaches in terms of what information can be collected, and what is the best way of doing so. However it is good manners, and standard practice, to inform each consultant that you are also inviting proposals from others.

Briefing the consultant
When you have identified who you intend to approach, you will be expected to provide them with a brief — in other words a statement providing as much information as possible about the problem you wish to have investigated. The brief should include:
- background information about your company — its product range, current markets and so on;
- a precise statement of your objectives in doing the research;
- some indication of the time-scale you require for completion;
- some indication of the financial constraints you wish to adhere to.

It is also useful at this early stage to clarify:
- whether or not you want the consultant to make recommendations on how you should proceed, based on the results of the research;
- whether you may require ongoing advice on how to implement these recommendations;
- whether or not you require interim reports while the research is being carried out.

Evaluating the proposal
The consultant or agency will subsequently provide you with a specific proposal, which should include:
- the objectives of the project
- the information which will be collected
- the research methods to be used — for example, the number of interviews planned, who is to be interviewed and how they will be selected
- the timetable for the project — how many days or weeks have been allocated to each stage of the project, and the specific dates on which you will receive interim reports and a final report

- the staff who will be involved. Sometimes the senior person who has sold you the research is not involved in carrying it out, and this task is delegated to a more junior person. It is not unreasonable that you should be informed of the name, qualifications and experience of the researcher primarily responsible for your job.
- the total costs, broken down in some detail to show for example staff time, travelling expenses, data processing and so on.

On the question of costs, it is quite common for a consultant to ask for part-payment in stages before the project is completed. A request that you agree to pay one-third of the total fee on commissioning the project, one-third on completion of fieldwork and one-third on receipt of the final report would not be at all abnormal.

Do not be afraid to seek clarification of any aspect of the proposal you have received, or to ask for it to be revised if you are not happy with it. Danger signs to watch out for are vagueness and lack of precision — the proposal should tell you exactly, but *exactly*, what information you will receive, how it will be collected, when you will get it, and how much it will cost.

USING THE INFORMATION

There is no point whatever in spending the time, effort and money needed to do market research unless you make good use of the information you have collected. This is so obvious that it seems scarcely worth mentioning — but it is a fact that many small firms make this elementary mistake. It is essential that you consider carefully the implications of what you have discovered, and incorporate the lessons it suggests into your forward planning. This might only involve making relatively small adjustments to some aspects of your day-to-day marketing activities, for example improving your packaging, or designing a better sales catalogue or brochure. On the other hand, it could lead to a radical reappraisal of your overall marketing strategy in the light of the new market trends and opportunities you have identified.

One final point — doing research should be an ongoing, continuous activity. It is not wise to relax and become complacent, safe in the knowledge that you have done your research. The needs of your customers and the activities of your competitors are changing all the time. It is highly likely that what was true eighteen months ago is no longer valid today. You have to keep up with the rest of the field if you want to be a winner!

Summary of Key Points
1. Doing market research involves collecting and using information which is useful in planning your company's marketing activities. You need information about your customers, your competitors, your own performance, and about the overall business environment.
2. You need to know who your actual and potential customers are, and what factors affect their purchasing decisions. You also need to know where, when and how they buy.
3. You need to know who your competitors are, and their strengths and weaknesses compared with your own operation.
4. You need to know what kind of reputation you have with your existing customers, and whether potential customers know that you exist.
5. You need to be aware of changes in the overall business environment so that you can adapt to changing circumstances.
6. Doing market research need not be outrageously expensive; you can find a lot of the information you need quite easily. Ways of doing this include getting hold of your competitors' sales catalogues, and by reading the trade press and special features in quality newspapers or magazines. You can also obtain much useful information from directories of one kind or another, and from government departments and industrial development agencies. Your own company records are also a valuable source of information.
7. You can acquire a great deal of valuable information simply by keeping your eyes and ears open as you walk round a supermarket, a trade fair or an exhibition. Simple observation of what your competitors are doing is a very useful and cost-effective research technique.
8. You can also collect information by doing interviews, but you must make sure that the people you contact are truly representative of the group you want to find out about. You also need to interview enough of them to make sure you are not being misled, but you will usually find that a consistent pattern begins to emerge fairly quickly.
9. You can discover a lot by test marketing a new product or service — in other words, by introducing it on a limited scale for a short period of time in a restricted geographical area.
10. Commissioning market research from an agency may be necessary if you do not have the time or expertise to do it yourself. You need to choose a reputable agency and brief them thoroughly on exactly what you want to find out. You should also investigate to see if you can obtain grant aid from one of the government bodies which assist small firms.

11. It is completely pointless to spend the time, effort and money needed to do market research unless you actually use the information you have collected.

A Case History

A small-scale furniture manufacturer who also operated five retail outlets in various parts of the country felt that he needed to do some market research. He wanted to find out:
- the catchment area for each of his stores
- what sort of people were buying which of his products
- whether there was any seasonality in the pattern of demand.

He was prepared to spend some money to commission a market research agency to work on the project, but he was persuaded to let an intelligent but fairly junior member of his office staff tackle the job. Using the companies' existing records and with a little bit of guidance, she was able to discover most of what he wanted to know. To determine the catchment area for each outlet, she used a large-scale map of the area and a box of coloured pins. Using back invoices and delivery notes, and a different colour pin for various types of furniture (red for dining room, green for bedroom, and so on), she simply put a pin in the map at the various addresses to which goods had been delivered during the previous twelve months. In that way, she soon built up a very useful and comprehensive picture of what was happening at each outlet. Local knowledge of the various neighbourhoods supplemented by informal chats with sales staff in the retail outlets was sufficient to provide the required information on the type of customer being attracted to each store. Further simple analysis of the delivery notes provided the answers to the seasonality question.

A Case History

A few years ago, a small co-operative creamery installed new equipment which, among other things, enabled it to produce a flavoured UHT (long-life) milk drink. The management committee gave the manager a month to draw up a detailed report with recommendations on whether or not to proceed with the proposal to develop a new product of this kind.

After scratching his head for a while, the manager drew up a list of questions he would need answered before he could write the required report. The basic issue, of course, was to find out whether or not there was a market for this kind of product. If the answer was yes, than a whole new series of supplementary questions arose, including:

- What sort of competition are we likely to face?
- What type and size of pack do we need?
- What price should we charge?
- What flavour should we produce?
- What quantities of each flavour?
- Would retailers be prepared to stock it?

The manager contacted a big market research agency, but was appalled at the price they quoted to provide the answers he needed. He decided to adopt a DIY approach. He already knew a number of buyers and store managers in his local area, so he went along to discover their views on the matter. He was surprised to find that, after meeting with three or four of them, he had most of the information he needed. One piece of information he was still unsure about — would his product be acceptable to the consumer?

After a few false starts, he was able to produce something very close to the final product, in three flavours — strawberry, banana and chocolate. He did not have the packaging sorted out at this stage, so he simply presented the samples in disposable plastic cups with a cling-film cover. He took them along to the local school at break time and handed them out to the kids (he had, of course, previously obtained the agreement of the headmistress). This simple consumer test proved that the product was acceptable, and indeed gave some useful indications on the relative popularity of the different flavours. Just to make sure, he repeated the exercise in several other schools in the area.

The new product was eventually launched on the market and proved to be a great success. Some years later, they did commission some 'proper' market research; the answers they obtained were not very different from those which had resulted from the DIY approach.

4.
Deciding What to Sell

Your decisions about what products or services you should offer are of fundamental importance to your survival prospects. These decisions influence just about every other aspect of your business — the size of your premises, the number of people you employ, your capital requirement and so on. If what you decide to offer is not what your customers want to buy, your chances of staying in business are nil. This basic principle of marketing — find out what the customers want and provide it for them — is all very well in theory. But in practice most small firms are already committed to their existing product range, at least in the short term. This is not necessarily a problem, provided you realise that you don't have to continue indefinitely with what you are offering at present. If all the available evidence suggests that customer demand for whatever it is you provide is disappearing like snow off a ditch on a sunny spring morning, the most sensible thing you can do is forget it — cut your losses, withdraw gracefully and try something else! However a more likely scenario is that your research will have given you some good ideas on how you might develop or adapt what you are currently offering to bring it more into line with the ever-changing requirements of your customers. This ability to change direction fairly quickly and easily is probably the most important advantage small firms have over their larger competitors.

There are a number of factors you need to bear in mind when you are making decisions about what to sell.

- What exactly do you mean by the product?
- Are services and products different?
- How do your products compare with your competitors?
- How many different products should you offer?
- How should you go about developing new products?

WHAT IS A PRODUCT?

You may think that this is a fairly stupid question to ask — everybody knows a product when they see one! But there is rather more to it than that. In one sense, a product is a tangible, physical entity — something you can see, touch and use. But there are also intangible elements associated with every product. Take, for example, a situation in which two competing firms are selling the same range of imported machinery. The specification and performance of the equipment supplied may be exactly the same in both cases. But assume that Company A can provide early delivery, 'free' installation and a speedy and efficient after-sales repair and maintenance service. Company B provides none of these additional benefits. All other things (like price) being equal, or nearly equal, which of these two suppliers is the customer more likely to prefer? The answer is obvious — most prospective customers will choose Company A. From the customer's point of view, these optional extras are an important part of the product. Taking a different example, why are housewives generally willing to pay several pence more for a tin of beans or a packet of biscuits which has a nationally-known brand name on the wrapper as opposed to a similar product in a retailer's 'own-label' wrapper? There is at least one food product currently available in Ireland where the outer wrapper is the *only* difference between the two brands — the actual physical contents of the pack are exactly the same. The explanation for this apparently illogical behaviour is that customers believe that one brand is in some sense better than the other, and this justifies them in paying the extra price. Quite often in consumer markets, the differences between different versions of the same basic product are more imaginary than real, and are the result of clever advertising over a fairly long period of time. If you think about it, it is not too difficult to draw up a fairly lengthy list of the intangible elements that might be associated with a product. These would include:

- the aesthetic appeal of its design/styling/packaging
- the prestige or status associated with using it
- whether it is regarded as fashionable or out-of-date
- whether or not it possesses some other desirable attribute (e.g. it is 'healthy')
- the availability or otherwise of a delivery, installation and maintenance service
- financing arrangements

Not all of these are appropriate to every product — but the basic point is very simple.

A PRODUCT IS EVERYTHING THE CUSTOMERS GET FOR THEIR MONEY.

There is one other point you need to remember. If every version of a product was exactly the same as every other one available on the market at a particular time, then the only rational way for consumers to choose between them would be on the basis of price. In that situation, the competition between different suppliers would be reduced to a battle to see who could offer the lowest price. Having to charge a higher cost, smaller suppliers would gradually but inevitably be forced out, and eventually the market would be dominated by one or two very large and efficient suppliers. The only way out of this dilemma which the smaller firm cannot hope to win is to make your product different from those of your competitors, giving customers a reason to prefer your particular version of it. You can do this in a multitude of ways, with a little bit of imagination and without spending a great deal of money. Some of the more obvious things you can do include the following.

- Give your product a distinctive and easily-remembered name. This will make it easier for you to establish its separate identity.
- Make some marginal differences to the physical appearance and/or the actual make-up of the product.
- Make sure that the packaging and presentation of your product is such that it stands out from the others in a way which will attract the attention of potential buyers.

Some examples of how small companies can do this might be helpful. A manufacturer of pork sausages felt he was losing out because customers could not really distinguish between his product and that of his competitors. After doing some market research (which sounds very grand — in this case it means that he talked to some retailers and a few housewives), he discovered that the average customer in his area preferred a fairly big sausage, and that she usually bought about ten at one go to keep the whole family happy. Our hero proceeded to make up packs of ten sausages wrapped in cling film on a polystyrene tray, with a label identifying them as 'Big Tens'. This actually worked very well in terms of increased sales.

Another example, just to illustrate that the importance of packaging and presentation is not confined to the consumer market, is the case of the small firm which manufactured agricultural machinery. A particular product was not selling very well. The first thing noted by a consultant called in by a government agency to give some advice was that the equipment was painted all over in a fairly boring colour (matt black, believe it or not). 'You'll need to do something about that, for a start,' said the consultant. 'It looks dreadful.'

'What for?' said the engineer.

'To make it look better.'

'What for?'

'Because people will be put off the minute they clap eyes on it. Paint it a different colour.'

'Sure, that won't make a blind bit of difference to its performance.'

'I know that, but it'll look better.'

After a lengthy and prolonged debate along these lines, the engineer was persuaded to respray the hopper and the engine casing bright yellow, and the rest of it bright blue. (These colours were selected totally on the spur of the moment.) He gradually acknowledged that this very simple product modification did make the machine much more attractive to look at, but it was not until much later that he had the grace to admit that there had been a significant improvement in the amount of interest shown by potential buyers at shows and in his own showroom.

Now, of course, it is not suggested that people are so gullible that they will buy a machine simply because it looks good. They will buy it because it is a well-designed and attractively-priced piece of equipment which they have been persuaded could do a good job for them. The point of the story is that their initial interest was stimulated by the very simple device of making the product stand out a little bit from the crowd.

It would be well worth the effort involved if you were to give some thought to how you could make your products just that little bit different.

PRODUCTS AND SERVICES

A lot of confusion is caused by the differences between products and services. Some people will tell you that these are so great that you need to apply a completely different set of guidelines to the marketing of a service. These differences include:

- The fact that many services are basically intangible. It is not possible to taste, feel, see, hear or smell the benefit you get from being insured, or from having your meal served by a polite and efficient waiter.
- The production and consumption of a service often occurs at the same moment. For example, you cannot produce a haircut and store it until someone wishes to buy it. Most goods are produced, then sold, and then consumed. Most services are sold, then produced and consumed at the same time.

- It is much more difficult to guarantee consistent quality in a service industry. Once you have set up a production line to manufacture a particular product, you can be reasonably certain that every item produced will be identical. In contrast, there can be a very wide variation in the overall quality of a particular service provided by different employees, and even from one occasion to the next with a single employee. Many franchise operations, such as fast-food outlets, try to ensure a uniformly high level of service by applying strict rules to every aspect of the business, but even then wide differences in quality can arise.
- As a broad general rule, products are moved from where they are manufactured to where the customer wishes to use them. Many services can only be provided in a particular location to which customers must come if they wish to purchase the service in question.
- Most services require a much higher level of contact between employees and customers than is the case with most manufactured goods.

However, although products and services are different in many ways, you should remember that many products also include a substantial service element. If you buy a new carpet, or a new exhaust system for your car, the deal may well include 'free' fitting. If you buy a photocopier for your office, you assume that its installation and subsequent maintenance are part of the overall purchase. Conversely, many services include a substantial product element within them — for example, hiring a car, or a hotel room, or buying a seat on an aircraft. In fact, the distinction between products and services is often so blurred that it is scarcely worth making. In practice, the principles of effective marketing apply equally to both products and services. Every product is slightly different, so that general principles need to be adapted by the individual manager and applied to his or her specific situation. The marketing of a service is just one more example of this.

THE SAME BASIC PRINCIPLES APPLY TO THE MARKETING OF BOTH PRODUCTS AND SERVICES.

HOW DO YOUR PRODUCTS COMPARE?

Your customers do not make decisions to buy or not to buy your product in a vacuum. They do so on the basis of their comparisons with the alternatives offered by your competitors. They make these comparisons on their assessment of how well each of the various alternatives cur-

rently available on the market match up to their requirements in terms of their:
- fitness for use
- general attractiveness
- psychological appeal
- reputation
- price

The basic requirement that has to be met when you are buying anything is that it will do the job that you want done. You would not buy a box of matches unless you believed that they will actually light when you strike them; nor would you buy them if you thought there was any risk that they would ignite spontaneously in your pocket. The same principle applies to more complex products, and indeed to services of all kinds. The only difference is that the criteria used to evaluate their performance will also be more complex. Customers assess a food product on such criteria as its taste, texture and nutritional value. A piece of machinery is judged on its technical performance and specification, and on things like its running costs, durability, reliability and so on.

As well as these purely functional aspects, customers also compare products using factors which are more difficult to define, mainly because they are subjective — what one person finds attractive might make someone else feel positively ill. This category of general appearance includes design, style, packaging and overall presentation. In addition, some products or services have an emotional or psychological appeal based on rather vague feelings of status, prestige, respectability or whatever associated with their purchase and use.

The reputation of a product

It is also important to remember that customers make their evaluations of competing products on the basis on what they *believe* to be true, which is not necessarily the same as what is actually true. Products and services and companies have a reputation, whether they like it or not. A good or a bad reputation will have a major influence on customers' purchasing decisions. You should take steps to find out what kind of reputation your products have compared with those of your competitors — you can so this by simply asking around. Even better, get someone else to do it for you — that way will avoid the problem of people telling you what they think you want to hear. If you should find out that your products, or your company as a whole, are not regarded very highly by potential customers, there is absolutely no point in sitting around moaning about it. You should try to find out whether your poor reputation is deserved in the light of your actual performance, and *do* something about it. If you discover that most people think that a particular machine you supply breaks down far more often than the alternative models offered by other suppliers, you can very easily carry out a check to see if this is true or not. Even if you can prove that it is not true, you still need to take corrective action by ensuring that customers know the facts rather than the rumours. This might require, for example, emphasising in your publicity material the proven reliability of your product in comparison with the others.

All of these different dimensions are weighed up by the customer against price, including not only the stated purchase price but also other price-related dimensions — discounts, easy payment terms, trade-in allowances and so on. However it is important to remember that most customers do not buy solely on price. They buy on the basis of what they regard as value for money. In other words, they somehow or other measure the price they are being asked to pay against all the benefits they will get if they decide to part with their money. They will choose the product which, in their judgment, offers the best costs-to-benefits ratio — and that is quite often *not* the cheapest version available on the market.

Compare your products with the competition

It is actually very enlightening to do a detailed analysis of how your products compare with those of your competitors under each of these headings. Assuming that you already know who your main competitors are (and if you don't, you really ought to find out pretty quickly), it is not difficult to carry out this kind of comparative assessment. You can do so simply by taking a blank sheet of paper and writing along the top the names of the two or three companies you regard as your major competitors, and then listing down the left-hand side the various factors noted above (or some variation of them which is more appropriate to your kind of business). All you have to do then is fill in the blanks! But you must be as objective as possible about it — there is no point whatsoever in kidding yourself that things are other than they actually are. If you do a comparison along these lines, you will almost certainly discover some areas where you are at a disadvantage, and others where you score better than the opposition. The lesson is obvious — play to your strengths when you are talking to potential customers, and try to do something about correcting your weaknesses.

You may also conclude that there is quite a wide range between the various alternatives available in terms of their price, quality and so on.

This is entirely consistent with the notion of different segments in the market requiring different versions of the same basic product. Take a pair of pliers as a very simple example. A professional electrician would probably buy something fairly expensive, which is likely to last a long time and stand up to heavy and continuous daily use. The home handyman or woman would probably buy something much cheaper, but adequate for changing a plug now and then. You should give some thought to where your products (or your services) are positioned within the overall market. Are you essentially a high quality/high price operator, or do you fit better into the lower quality/lower price end of the market? Or are you trying to do both with different versions of essentially the same basic product? Are there any obvious gaps in the market which you could fill?

The important thing to remember is that this is not just a matter of chance. Your positioning within the market is your decision. You should make that decision in the light of what you know about what the customer wants, what your competitors are doing, and what you yourself are capable of doing with the expertise and resources available to you.

HOW MANY PRODUCTS?

There are two things you need to bear in mind when you are thinking about this particular issue.

- It is usually unwise to rely on a single product.
- No product lasts forever.

The risks involved in being a single-product company are fairly obvious — you will rapidly find yourself in serious difficulties if for any reason the demand for your sole product begins to decline. It makes sense to spread the risk by developing a range of products, provided that you take care to avoid overstretching your resources to a point where you create cash flow problems for yourself by trying to do too much too quickly. You can begin the process of widening your product range by trying to answer two questions based on what you are doing at present.

- Could you offer your existing customers a variation of your existing product?
- Can you think of any other group of customers who might buy your existing product if it was presented in a slightly different way?

THE LIFE CYCLE OF A PRODUCT

Just like human beings, products and services are born, grow to maturity, and eventually die. Think back to your childhood — how many of the basic household and confectionary products you can remember are still around? Maybe quite a few — but many of them are long since gone. On the other side of the coin, how many products and services which are now commonplace simply did not exist when you were a child? The basic reason for this steady turnover is that new products and services are coming onto the market all the time. Many of them fall at the first hurdle, but some of them succeed. As sales of a new product increase, older established products find it more difficult to attract customers. Eventually they may be forced off the market altogether. The new product then becomes established, and is highly successful for a while. Eventually and inevitably, it will in its turn be replaced by a new entrant. In other words, every product goes through a life cycle involving a number of clearly recognisable stages — birth, growth, maturity and decline. There is considerable variation in the actual length of time which products take to pass through the various stages of their life. A pop record may complete the entire cycle in a few months. A particular style or 'look' in the fashion trade may last for only a year or two. In contrast, the life of a particular type of car can be extended over thirty years or more — for example the Morris Minor and the Volkswagen Beetle. But the basic lesson still holds — sooner or later, your existing product will become obsolete and will be replaced by something new. So thinking about what you are going to offer in five years' time is not an optional extra — it is a vital necessity for every small firm.

Figure 5. The life cycle of a product

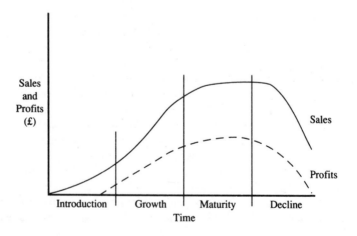

NEW PRODUCTS

Launching a new infant product onto the market is always a difficult and risky undertaking. Above all else, you must not make the elementary mistake of developing a new product before you are absolutely certain that there is a market for it, and you have a fairly precise idea of what the customer wants. Do your research first and then develop and launch your new product — not the other way round. This will reduce substantially your chances of ending up with a costly failure on your hands. It is always a little bit sad to hear someone say 'But it's a good product — people *ought* to want it — I can't understand why it's not selling.' The fact that you have a very good product is totally irrelevant if nobody wants to buy it — but this kind of thing happens all the time. Incidentally, it is not only small firms which fall into this particular trap. Few people would dispute the fact that the supersonic airliner Concorde is a superb engineering achievement. We are still impressed by the fact that it is able to fly people from London to Washington in less than four hours. The only problem with Concorde is that the customers (in this case, the major airlines) are not prepared to buy it — they prefer a product which can fly a substantially greater number of passengers a little more slowly but at a much lower cost per seat/mile.

Even if you get it right, you should not expect a new product to be immediately profitable. It is actually quite unusual to be in the black right from Day One. Breaking even is a much more realistic target in the early stages, and you should not be surprised or discouraged if you make a loss for a while. What you should do, of course, is to build that possibility into your budget, and count it as part of the total investment required to launch the new product successfully. The basic reason for this is that your revenue is at its lowest just at the moment when your costs are highest. You have already spent money on development, perhaps bought new equipment and certainly purchased the materials you need. As well as these initial costs, your overheads will be spread over a relatively low level of output, and you will not yet have had the time to iron out the bugs which inevitably crop up in the production and distribution system. You will also have to spend some money on advertising and sales promotion. At the same time, the volume of sales will be low, and in consequence the amount of money coming in is unlikely to be sufficient to cover your costs. So do not despair too soon — but if sales do not begin to pick up, you will eventually have to make the difficult decision to cut your losses and get out while the going is good.

MATURE PRODUCTS

On a more optimistic note, if you have done your homework well and the new product catches on, there will then be a period of fairly rapid growth in terms of sales volume. Profits should begin to improve substantially as sales revenue increases and costs per unit of output begin to fall. However you can be sure that if you end up in that happy position, others will have noticed it. Sooner or later they will start looking for a piece of the action.

Primarily because of gradually increasing competition, sales will eventually begin to level off, or continue to grow but only very slowly. The most likely outcome is a period of relative stability, during which sales volume, costs and profits are fairly predictable. Profit margins tend to be squeezed due to intensified competitive pressure, with fairly uniform price levels being charged by all suppliers. In this mature stage of a product's life cycle, companies often try to boost their sales by actively searching for:

- new uses for the product
- new users for the product
- ways to persuade existing users to increase their usage rate

Many mature products are around for a very long time — the example of the Volkswagen Beetle has already been noted. However the key point to remember is that it is absolutely certain that sales of a given product will eventually begin to fall sooner or later. The decline may be so sudden and rapid that it is a total catastrophe for the small company, involving all that word implies in terms of damage and danger. In some cases the decline takes place quite slowly, creeping up on you so that you hardly notice it until it is too late. The problem in this situation is that it is very difficult to decide at the time whether a reduction in sales is only temporary, or represents the beginning of a long-term irreversible decline. The basic reason why you can be sure that a given product will in the end get to this stage in its life cycle is that somebody, somewhere, sometime, will come up with an alternative which your customers will regard as better in some sense. When that happens, a positive decision has to be taken, which usually boils down to choosing among three possible alternatives:

- Cease production immediately.
- Decrease production in line with decreasing sales.
- Re-launch the product.

The first of these options often presents difficulties for the smaller firm. Quite often you find that the company has been built primarily on the success of one particular product. In this situation, it is extremely difficult to accept that times have changed and the product is no longer the jewel in your crown, but an increasing liability. This is one of the times when sentiment has to go out the window. If the logic of your balance sheet suggests that a particular product has had its day, you simply cannot afford to keep it on board just for old times' sake. A gradual reduction in output as sales decrease is sometimes not possible for technical reasons — you either run the production line at a certain capacity, or you don't run it at all. However in some cases it is feasible to reduce output relatively slowly and phase the product out over a long period of time. If you choose this option, you should try to maximise your profits by avoiding any unnecessary expenditure on technical development, advertising and sales promotion — in other words, you should milk it dry. Re-launching a declining product is difficult, risky and expensive. It can be done, but you need to very sure of your ground before attempting it.

You should take a good look at your current product range and try to work out roughly what stage each product is at in terms of its life-cycle. If you conclude that they are all in the mature stage, you should recognise this as a warning sign rather than a matter for congratulations. Even though sales may be going very well indeed at the moment, you have to ask yourself what is likely to happen in the next few years. Many companies, including some major multinationals, have found themselves in serious difficulties through allowing all their products to go out-of-date at more or less the same time. A company in that position is very vulnerable. You need to take positive action to ensure that you have a balanced portfolio of products which includes what somebody once referred to as 'tomorrow's breadwinners' in addition to those which account for the great bulk of your sales, and your profits, today. In other words, to guarantee your survival in the longer term, you need to give some thought to the possibility of developing new products.

DEVELOPING NEW PRODUCTS

It is quite wrong to think that a new product must always be a major technological breakthrough, something which simply did not exist before. There are, of course, plenty of examples of this kind of new product which have emerged over the last twenty years or so — the video recorder, the microwave oven, the digital watch, the personal computer. Each of these was the outcome of a massive investment of time and money in research and development, and subsequently in production and marketing. Developing this kind of new product is usually far beyond the capabilities of any small business — but that is not a valid reason for believing that small firms can never hope to launch any new products of any kind.

Consider for a moment what exactly is meant by a 'new' product. When you think about it, you will realise that the easiest way to define a 'new' product is quite simply as something which the majority of potential buyers believe to be new. If everybody thinks it's new, then it's new! The great majority of 'new' products are not the outcome of a major technological breakthrough; in fact they are not truly new at all in the strictest sense of the word. As far as you and your firm are concerned, a 'new' product can be:

- a fairly minor modification of an existing product (e.g. different packaging);
- your version of a competitor's successful product or service; or
- a product or service which is new to this country, but has been around elsewhere for years (e.g. the continental quilt, the pizza parlour).

The actual process of developing a new product or service need not depend on the flash of inspiration one fine day. There are a number of logical steps involved which are not difficult to follow.

- Identify possibilities.
- Evaluate their potential.
- Develop and test the actual product.
- Test the market.
- Organise a full-scale launch.

Identifying possibilities

Ideas for possible new products can come from a wide variety of sources, including:

- feedback from customers
- the activities of competitors
- study of technical/trade journals
- awareness of developments in other countries
- using your imagination and your knowledge of trends in the market

One specific technique you may have heard of is called 'brainstorming'. It simply means sitting down with a few colleagues or friends for an hour or so and deliberately trying to churn out some new ideas without worrying too much at that stage whether or not they are likely to work.

Deciding What to Sell 57

Evaluating potential
However at a very early stage, you will have to put these various possibilities through some kind of screening process to eliminate those which are not really feasible for one reason or another. You should not be surprised or discouraged when you find that you end up rejecting most of your new ideas. This is quite normal, and it is far better to sort out the non-starters before you spend a lot of time and money on them. It also makes a lot of sense to use a standard check-list so as to ensure that you are applying the same criteria all the time. You will have to work out a check list which is appropriate to your own operation, but as an absolute minimum, it should include:

- market potential
- resources required
- competitive reaction

Your starting point has to be an estimate of whether or not a sufficient number of buyers is likely to be attracted to the new product. Your review of market potential should also include such things as long-term growth prospects, the likely stability or seasonality of demand, preliminary estimates of the price range which customers would find acceptable, and the existence or otherwise of possible alternatives. It is also essential to make sure at a very early stage that the resources likely to be required are not beyond your reach. This will involve thinking about whether or not you will need to purchase new equipment or move to larger premises or increase your workforce. Do you have the technical ability required or can you acquire it? What is the availability of the materials you will need, and what is likely to be the cost of buying them in the quantities you will need? You should try to bring all of those elements together into a statement of the total amount of money you are likely to need — and then ask yourself where you are going to get it. Last but by no means least, you need to think about how many competitors you are likely to come up against, what their strengths and weaknesses are, and how they are likely to react. At the end of the day, you are really trying to come up with some kind of costs-to-benefits ratio to enable you to judge whether or not it is worth going ahead. Included in that decision should be the fact that the money you invest in this particular project will not be available for other purposes, and you will have to decide whether that is in line with your overall objectives and needs.

Developing and testing
Once you have taken a firm decision to go ahead, the next step is to create a few prototypes of the new product. In the early stages, this is

essentially a technical problem, and for that reason it is difficult to lay down hard and fast rules other than to say that it must be solved within the constraints set by:
- the technical capabilities of the company
- the known needs and preferences of potential customers
- the financial limits of the available budget

When this has been done, it is essential to undertake an intensive programme of product testing to make sure that the new product conforms to its specifications in terms of performance and reliability. Here again, the detail will be different for different kinds of products. In the case of a new food product, product testing may also involve the use of consumer panels to ensure that its taste, texture and method of preparation are acceptable, as well as laboratory testing of packaging, shelf life and so on. A piece of machinery will often be tested virtually to destruction by prolonged running at optimum speed. At this stage, too, the various legal requirements should be identified and steps taken to ensure that these are fully met.

Testing the market

Test marketing can be defined as launching the product on a limited scale in a small part of the total market. The object of the exercise is to identify and correct weaknesses either in the product itself or in the way in which it is marketed (e.g. the choice of outlets) before you go into full-scale production. Test marketing is not really feasible for some kinds of products, and even where it is feasible, it may not always be wise. The big drawback is that you are showing your hand to the competition, and thus giving them the chance to react quickly. There is at least one well documented case of a firm which test marketed a confectionery product only to find that a competitor's copy was launched before their own market test was completed.

Full-scale launch

Launching a new product onto the market is a major operation which requires careful and detailed planning. As an absolute minimum, it is essential that you take steps to ensure that:
- adequate supplies are available in appropriate outlets;
- adequate production capacity has been set aside to fulfil new orders as they arise;
- appropriate promotional activity has been undertaken so that potential customers are aware of what is happening;
- after-sales service arrangements are in place.

Deciding What to Sell

A full-scale national launch of a new consumer product can cost several million pounds, and that kind of effort is clearly beyond the scope of most small firms. However, even on a more limited scale, you need to put a lot of effort into making sure that your new product gets off to the best possible start.

Summary of Key Points
1. It is entirely your decision which products and services you choose to offer your customers. But remember that customers' needs and wants are changing all the time. You don't have to continue indefinitely with what you are offering at present. In fact, the ability to change direction fairly quickly and easily in response to changing circumstances is probably the most important single advantage small firms have over their larger competitors.
2. A product is everything the customers get for their money — including the intangible elements such as its aesthetic appeal, or the status associated with using it, or the availability of a delivery, installation and maintenance service.
3. People will decide to buy your product on the basis of the comparisons with the alternatives offered by your competitors. You need to make your version of a particular product or service distinctively different from its competitors in some way—otherwise customers have no rational basis for buying from you other than a low price. There are many possible ways of making your offering stand out from the crowd. These include giving it a brand name and making sure it is packaged and presented attractively.
4. There are some ways in which a service is obviously different from a product, but the same basic principles apply to the marketing of both products and services.
5. It is usually unwise to rely completely on a single product, and no product lasts forever. You need to think about developing new products to broaden your range and to remain competitive in the longer term.
6. A new product does not have to be a major technological advance. Most 'new' products are merely modifications of existing products, or your version of a competitor's successful product, or a product new to this country (but which has been around for years elsewhere).
7. Before you introduce a new product or service, you must evaluate its market potential and make absolutely certain that you can produce it in bulk to a consistently high standard without going bank-

rupt. You may find it useful to test market it before going for a full-scale launch.
8. Just like human beings, all products and services are born, grow to maturity and eventually die. You should take a good look at your current range and try to work out roughly where each item is in terms of its life-cycle. You should not persist for sentimental reasons with a product which really is past it. You will be in trouble if all of your products go out-of-date at more or less the same time. You need to have a balanced product portfolio which includes 'tomorrow's breadwinners' as well as those which account for most of your sales and projects today.

A Case History
About ten years ago, two brothers set up a small firm making a food product for which there was a growing demand — fresh coleslaw salad, which they initially sold in unbranded fifty gram tubs through small retail outlets in their immediate area. The way in which they set about broadening their product range as their business grew is a good example of how the suggested thinking can be applied. It rapidly became apparent to them that, in addition to the domestic market, coleslaw would also be sold to hotels, restaurants, factory canteens and so on. In response, they developed the two kilogram catering pack. Again, housewives sometimes wish to buy a larger quantity for a special occasion, but the large catering pack was a bit much for this purpose — hence the 'family size' 500 gram pack. More recently, the company has begun to manufacture and pack 'own brand' versions of the product for multiple retailers and other food processing companies. Variations to the basic chilled salad were introduced progressively simply by varying the ingredients — American salad, potato salad and so on. In this simple way, the initial single product was adapted and broadened to meet the needs of different customer groups. Just as a matter of interest, the company now employs about 150 people.

5.
Setting a Price

In most small firms, prices are set by the company's accountant. Prices are based on a calculation of costs, plus a mark-up. It is assumed that the cost estimates used are more or less correct. The mark-up is usually based on what is the accepted custom and practice for that particular type of business. If these calculations result in a price which is too high in relation to what competitors are charging, and what customers expect to pay, then the price is modified downwards to take account of market conditions. Underlying this brief statement of what actually happens in most cases, there are a lot of issues which are worth looking at in more detail.

One of the most important is the fact that there is no such thing as 'the' price for anything. Different versions of a particular product are offered by different suppliers at different prices. Even in the case of a single supplier, different prices are often negotiated with different customers. Instead of thinking of 'the' price, you need to take on board right at the start the idea that for any good or service, there exists a range of possible prices within which customers and suppliers interact. The price which you choose to set is not fixed in tablets of stone as a result of a complicated bit of arithmetic. Price is a very powerful weapon in your overall armoury. You should use it consciously and positively to help you achieve your marketing objectives. Whether you decide to set your prices towards the lower end of the price range, somewhere in the middle, or at the upper end will depend on your analysis of all the many factors which are relevant. It is convenient to look at the various influences on a company's pricing policy under three broad headings:
- Customers
- Competitors
- Costs

CUSTOMERS
Some people make the major mistake of assuming that customers make their decisions to buy or not to buy a particular item solely on the basis

of its price. This is simply not true, and you only have to think about your own purchasing behaviour to see that. Imagine for a moment that you have decided to take your partner out to dinner. Would you go to the cheapest place you can think of in your local area? Would you wear the cheapest possible clothes you could find? Would you travel there and back by the cheapest possible mode of transport? If you have answered 'yes' to all three of these questions, it might be worth your while to seek professional advice before you destroy a perfect friendship! It is much more likely that your response was something along the lines that you would not choose the absolutely cheapest possible from all the alternatives available to you, but equally you would not choose the most expensive you could find unless, perhaps, it was a very special occasion and you were feeling particularly prosperous at the time. In other words, your buying behaviour is influenced by:

- the amount of money you have available to spend; and
- your personal views on what level of quality you would regard as acceptable.

This very simple example serves to illustrate a number of important points about pricing.

- Different customers will take a different view of what is an acceptable price, depending on how well off they are.
- Customers will compare your price, and what they get for it, with the price charged by your competitors.
- They will make their choice between a range of competing alternatives on the basis of what they believe is the best value for money when they weigh different factors — how much they can afford in conjunction with what they get in return.
- It is actually quite unusual for people to opt for the cheapest possible version of anything.

The importance of price to the customer

It is perhaps worth spending a little more time on this question of what people expect to get in return for paying the price asked. Let us return for a moment to the example of your own buying behaviour. When you are buying a new suit, for example, you will not only look at the price tag. You will also take into account such things as:

- the quality of the material, the cut, the stitching and so on;
- the overall style — whether it suits you or not, and whether or not it is fashionable;

- what it does for you in terms of the self-image you want to project to other people;
- how long it is likely to last.

Somehow or other, you will assess all of these factors in relation to the price and come up with your own ideas on whether you think a particular garment is good value for money or otherwise. When you have done this for a number of different suits, you will decide which of them offers the best overall value for money, and buy it. Moreover, this way of thinking about price does not apply only to customers' decisions about purchasing consumer goods such as clothing and foodstuffs. It also applies to buying industrial goods such as components and parts, machinery and equipment, except that in this case different non-price factors will influence the purchasing decision. These non-price factors include:

- performance
- reliability
- ease of maintenance
- availability and price of spare parts
- delivery
- after-sales service

In fact, a number of research studies have proved that if you ask buyers of industrial goods to rate the relative importance of these various elements in their overall purchasing decision, price comes well down the list in order of importance. The basic point you should keep in mind is actually a very simple one:

CUSTOMERS RARELY BUY SOLELY ON THE BASIS OF PRICE.

It is also worth remembering that you can actually set too low a price. If someone were to offer you a brand new 24-inch colour television set with a built-in video recorder for, let's say, £50, you would immediately be a little bit suspicious. Unless you are very naive indeed, you would think that either it was part of a consignment which had been helped to fall off the proverbial lorry, or alternatively that there was a fair chance of it blowing up, or breaking down, or otherwise ceasing to function after about a fortnight. These unkind thoughts would be entirely typical of how most people react to such an offer. This serves to illustrate another important aspect of pricing:

PRICE IS OFTEN TAKEN AS AN INDICATOR OF QUALITY.

The effect of price changes

There is one other aspect of pricing from the customer's point of view which you should be aware of. As a general rule, if the price of something goes up, people will buy less of it, and some people will stop buying it altogether. Conversely, if the price is reduced, people will tend to buy more, and some people who did not buy it in the past will start doing so. This broad rule of thumb about how customers react to price changes is not actually all that helpful in practice, because some goods and services are much more sensitive than others to price variations. In some cases, a fairly small increase in price will result in quite a large decrease in sales, and vice-versa — a small reduction in price will lead to a fairly substantial increase in sales. This can happen in one of two ways. First, it can happen right across the board — in other words, when every supplier raises or lowers their price by roughly the same amount at more or less the same time. Secondly, it can happen when one supplier raises or lowers his or her price while the others remain at the same level. Quite often you will find that the demand for a particular product is not very sensitive to a general price rise involving every supplier, but is very sensitive indeed to a price change on the part of only one supplier.

Petrol is quite a good example of this phenomenon. Most people regard their cars as necessities. They are prepared to buy the petrol they need to run it, regardless of regular steep increases in its price. The total sales of petrol in this country have not really been affected by price rises over the years, although there was a downturn for a while in the mid-1970s in response to the fairly horrendous one-off price increases which occurred at that time. But while sales of petrol in total are not very price sensitive, sales of a particular brand of petrol are extremely sensitive to very small price changes in a situation where the price of other brands is unchanged. You must have seen the queues of eager motorists outside petrol stations anxious to benefit from a few pence per gallon during the price-wars which flare up from time to time. The basic reason for this behaviour is that there is virtually no difference between the various brands of petrol available on the market — price is the only rational basis for choosing one brand rather than another. This is why the major oil companies avoid direct price competition like the plague, and compete for trade on the basis of trading stamps, free gifts and so on.

The sort of products which tend to be fairly sensitive to changes in their price are those which:

Setting a Price

- do not cost a lot per item;
- are purchased frequently in small quantities; and
- show very little difference between alternative versions of the same basic product.

Most of the things which tend to be much less sensitive to changes in their price are those which:

- are of high unit value — i.e. involve the customer in a fairly substantial outlay in relation to his/her income;
- are purchased relatively infrequently; and
- are distinctively different from alternative versions of the same basic product.

This category includes most consumer durables (fridges, freezers, washing machines and so on), as well as most kinds of machinery and equipment.

The same basic rules apply to services. The more unique and distinctively different a service is, the greater the scope for price variations without incurring the risk of a substantial decrease in demand.

It is worth asking yourself how sensitive your particular products are likely to be to changes in their price. Of course when you try this, you will soon discover that it is not really possible to answer this question without also thinking about your competitors.

COMPETITORS

It is so obvious that it is scarcely worth saying — but you really ought to know in some detail exactly what your competitors are charging. This does not necessarily mean that you should automatically come into line with them if you discover that their prices are significantly higher (or lower) than yours, but it is a fact that the price you can set will depend to some extent on the competition. A straightforward price comparison has to be the starting point of your analysis. You should also look at how your competitors compare with you in terms of their:

- packaging and presentation
- design and performance
- availability and delivery
- payment terms
- image and reputation

When you have done this, you will be in a much better position to decide your overall pricing strategy. You really have only three alternatives to choose from. You can decide as a matter of general policy to pitch your prices at a level which is:

- lower than most of your competitors
- about the same as most of your competitors
- higher than most of your competitors

Adopting a low-price strategy

General speaking, adopting a low-price strategy is not a good idea for the smaller firm. Most small firms which decide to take this option do so for one of three reasons.

- They mistakenly believe that customers buy solely on price.
- They have no alternative due to severe price competition.
- They believe that, by doing so, they can grab a slice of the market from their competitors.

Competing on price

We have already discussed, and hopefully knocked firmly on the head, the notion that customers buy solely on price. All the available evidence suggests that this is simply not true. However some markets where there is very little to choose between different versions of the same basic product can be very price-sensitive. Sometimes this situation arises due to cheap foreign imports, or where a very large competitor has substantial excess production capacity which must be utilised. If you should find yourself in that position, the only sensible way out is to identify and emphasise to customers the non-price features and benefits you can offer, and hope that these are sufficient to justify charging a slightly higher price. You will need to work at it, and think seriously about adapting your product so that it is in fact distinctively different from the rest in some way — quality, design, personal service or whatever.

The alternative is to try and match the opposition blow for blow. Nearly always this is a contest which the small firm can never win. It implies cost reductions which you cannot hope to achieve with a small-scale operation located in a relatively high-wage economy. The best advice that can be given to someone in that situation is to cut your losses, get out while the going is good and try something else. This should not be regarded as a major personal defeat, nor is there any reason to be ashamed of it. On the contrary, it is a rational and sensible business decision to utilise your capital and your expertise in an area where you are more likely to be successful, rather than to wear yourself out trying to achieve the impossible. The first and most basic objective of any business is to survive. And if you conclude that you cannot survive in the long term in your present line of business, there is no virtue whatsoever in struggling on against ever-increasing odds.

Building market share

Using price as a weapon to try and build up your market share is not usually a good idea either. You need to reach a certain level of profit in order to make a living for yourself and to generate some of the funds you will need to expand the business. You can earn the same amount of profit by selling a relatively low volume at a high profit margin per unit, or by selling a high volume at a lower profit margin per unit. Attempting to increase your share of the market by pursuing a low-price strategy implies accepting the second of these two approaches as the basis of your business. You should carefully think through what that implies in practice. For high volume sales, you need to have adequate production capacity. To earn any decent profit margin, you need to keep your costs to an absolute minimum. This implies operating your plant to near maximum levels of output at maximum efficiency over a prolonged period of time. This is actually quite difficult to do, as you may have discovered already. In any event, you would have very little spare cash available for such things as advertising. The biggest problem of all is that, in a geographically small market such as Ireland, a high volume of sales almost certainly means getting hold of quite a substantial share of the market. This will inevitably draw you to the attention of the big boys, and provoke a fierce competitive response once you get to a level where you are causing them any real damage. They are quite likely to react by starting a price war which you are unlikely to win because you do not have the financial reserves you would need to survive it.

Price cutting as a part of a short-term promotion (e.g. a 'special offer') can be useful, but you need to be careful. The basic difficulty is that once you have reduced your price for any reason, it is usually very difficult to get it back up again. Giving special discounts to a particular customer is also risky. People talk, and you will soon find that everyone is threatening to take their business elsewhere unless they get the same terms. Just about the only situation where price cutting can be justified without any qualification is when you need to clear out old stock, as you might do immediately before launching a new product.

Pricing at the same level as competitors

A strategy of setting your prices so as to remain more or less level with your competitors suffers from the drawback that you must also keep your costs in line with theirs if you are to maintain profitability. As we have already discussed, a situation might arise where the price competition is so severe that you simply cannot keep up with it. A completely different kind of risk is that you might be able to justify charging a higher price than your competitors, and by keeping on par with them you are simply losing potential profits. However it is wise to take a deliberate decision not to rock the boat if you believe either of the following:

- Your product or service is not all that distinctively different from the competitors.
- You would lose a substantial volume of business by stepping out of line.

Adopting a high-price strategy

As a broad general rule, increasing your prices inevitably means reducing the total amount you sell. There are a number of very sound reasons why it often makes sense for a small firm to adopt a policy of charging higher prices than most of its competitors, even though this may well mean remaining relatively small.

- Lower sales volume does not necessarily mean lower profits.
- A small firm is more likely to survive and prosper in the longer term if it operates on the basis of low volume/high price/high profit margin.
- It is easier to manage a small-scale operation than a large one.
- It is easier to retain control of a small-scale operation in the longer term.

The idea of deliberately sacrificing sales volume might seem to be rather stupid at first sight, but you should bear in mind that your primary objective is to achieve the level of profits you want. You can earn the same level of profits with radically different levels of output, depending on your profit margin. For example, you could earn £10,000 of profit with many different combination of sales volume and net profit per unit sold.

Number of Units Sold	Net Profit per Unit
20,000	£0.50
10,000	£1.00
5,000	£2.00
2,000	£5.00
500	£20.00

Your accountant will probably tell you that in the real world, the sums are a bit more complicated than this — but the basic principle still applies.

Setting a Price

Finding a niche

As we have already noted, small firms which choose to go down the high volume/low profit margin route generally find it extremely difficult to survive in the longer term. They usually fall victims to the competitive pressure exerted by larger companies operating at much higher levels of output. The cost savings which result from really large-scale production are such that smaller producers are soon squeezed out unless they can find a niche in the market which has been overlooked or ignored by their larger competitors. The best way to exploit such a niche is to provide a product or service which is specifically tailored to meet the needs of the relatively small group of customers concerned, and for which they are prepared to pay a premium price. This custom-built approach almost certainly implies higher production, distribution and marketing costs, which can only be sustained by a higher-than-average price. It may well also result in the business continuing to operate on quite a small scale almost indefinitely unless it can succeed in identifying and developing a number of different slots in the total market.

Keeping the business small has the further advantage that it is easier to manage. That statement needs a bit of explanation. Most people who have set up their own business would agree that it is a fairly traumatic experience. In the early stages, there is a lot of worry and lot of running about trying to do just about everything yourself (or so it seems at the time). Life becomes a lot easier once you have become established on a reasonably sound footing. There are still problems, of course, but they tend to be things you have encountered before and which you know how to deal with. The hassle starts up again in a really serious way if you try to expand. Once you increase your sales beyond a certain point, you will need more staff, more production capacity, more working capital — more problems of every kind. There is also the ever-present risk of over-trading — in other words, expanding too quickly. What usually happens is that you buy in new machinery and materials, take on extra staff and so on to enable you to fulfil a number of large new orders; you then find that you have to pay for them before your customers have paid you. If your bank manager is not very understanding, there is a real chance that you will end up in liquidation. Expanding the business may also require raising additional capital from external sources. This will almost certainly mean accepting some degree of external influence on your freedom to make your own managerial decisions. It may well mean losing control altogether of the business you have spent so much time and effort to create.

All of this should not be taken as an exhortation to remain small at all costs. It really does come down to your own personal value system. You may feel strongly that you want to retain control of your own ship — indeed the idea of working for yourself rather than somebody else may well have been why you decided to go into business on your own in the first place. On the other hand, you may relish the challenge of managing the expansion and development of your enterprise. But even if this is what you want to do, it still makes sense to set your prices at the highest level the market will bear, or to be more precise, that part of the overall market in which you have decided to operate. In order to grow, you will have to generate some capital from earnings, and this is only possible if you maximise your profits.

Justifying a higher price

The difficulty is that it is totally unrealistic to simply decide one fine day that you are going to charge a higher price than most of your competitors. You can only hope to do so if you can persuade a sufficient number of potential customers that it is worth paying that little bit extra for your particular offering. This implies that they must be able to see in it something distinctively different and valuable. That something can be:

- a real technical advantage
- higher quality
- better presentation
- better service

Every company is different. Before you try to raise your prices, you need to think carefully about what you can give the customers in return for their giving you their order.

COSTS

The traditional way to work out the price of a product is to calculate the total costs of manufacturing and distributing it and then add on a profit margin. The profit margin, or mark-up, is often set at a level which is considered to be what is normally accepted as standard for that kind of business. The main advantage of this approach is that it is easy to understand. It is also very familiar to most people with any kind of business experience, since this is still how the great majority of small firms in Ireland set their prices. Unfortunately, it suffers from two major drawbacks.

- Prices calculated in this way take no account of market conditions.
- It is assumed that costs can be estimated with a high degree of accuracy.

Setting a Price

In fairness, very few firms are daft enough to ignore what is happening in the market. The reason why you find very few firms which act in this way is that those which do tend to go out of business fairly quickly. Most firms modify their prices in some way in the light of what their competitors are charging for broadly similar goods or services.

Cost-plus pricing

The more serious problem is that it is actually very difficult to calculate costs accurately. What you have to remember is that when you (or your accountant) try to set a price, you are not working on facts. You are working on estimates of what you think is likely to happen in the future — and one of the things you can be absolutely certain about in this life is that the future is uncertain! A typical cost-based price calculation would look something like Figure 6.

Well before the start of the financial year, your accountant will ask you to forecast the likely level of sales over the next twelve months. If you are unable to provide him/her with this information, he/she simply makes a guess, based mainly on what he/she has calculated you will need to sell in order to stay in business and make a reasonable profit. The accountant then tries to estimate the total direct costs for both labour and materials. The next step is to estimate the likely total expenditure on indirect labour and materials, and on general overheads, for the firm as a whole. By definition, these are items that you cannot relate directly to any particular product. The wages you pay to the person who keeps your books on a day-to-day basis is an example of an indirect labour charge. The costs of the materials used to clean your office are obviously indirect. As well as things such as rent, rates, heat and light, the general overhead tends to be regarded as a general dumping ground for everything else on which the firm spends money—including, for example, the costs of running your car.

The accountant's dilemma is that all of these things have to be paid for out of your sales revenue and so they have to be included in your costs. But in all honesty there is no universally-accepted basis for sharing out these indirect costs between different products. The dilemma is usually resolved by charging them as a percentage of direct costs at a level which will fully recover them over a year's trading, provided that the forecast level of sales is achieved. The problem is that if sales turn out to be lower than forecast, general overheads and other indirect costs will not be fully recovered, and profits will suffer as a result. Conversely, if sales turn out to be higher than forecast, more overheads and other indirect costs will be recovered than is strictly necessary, and this will be reflected in a level of profits higher than was anticipated. Add to this the obvious fact that profits will also be affected if for any reason there is an unforeseen increase or decrease in your direct costs during the year.

Figure 6. A typical cost-plus price calculation

	£	£
Direct materials	5.00	
Direct labour	2.00	
Total direct cost		7.00
Indirect materials (say, 20% of direct materials)	1.00	
Indirect labour (say 25% of direct labour)	0.50	
General overheads (say, 40% of direct labour)	0.80	
Total indirect cost		2.30
Total cost		9.30
Profit margin (say, 33%)		3.10
List price		12.40

Managers of small firms who do not have any knowledge of accounting practices tend to assume that the cost statements which their accountants use to calculate a selling price are the absolute truth. They are nothing of the sort!

COST CALCULATIONS ARE ONLY APPROXIMATIONS.

The basic point of all this is to make you realise that it is not particularly sensible to decide your overall pricing strategy solely on the basis of these kinds of cost calculations. They are a very useful starting point, and it is not suggested that you should immediately throw them out of the window. But you only have to look at Figure 6 to see that you can radically alter the recommended selling price and/or the apparent profitability of a particular product simply by changing the percentages used to recover overheads and other indirect costs. This is how the very low prices of some foreign imports are sometimes made possible — the price is set on the basis of recovering 100 per cent of overheads on sales in the home market, so that export sales are priced solely on direct costs plus a profit margin. It is highly unlikely that you could go that far, but you should realise that you can apply the same kind of thinking and manipulate your prices to some extent by changing the allocation of your overheads between products.

Setting a Price

The break-even point

As an absolute minimum, you should calculate your 'break-even point'— i.e. the amount of product you will have to sell in a given period in order to fully recover your costs. The starting point is to estimate your total fixed costs (your 'overheads') for the period in question. By definition, these costs will remain unchanged regardless of the level of output achieved. Then estimate those costs which are directly linked to changes in output — principally materials and direct labour — and work out how they are likely to change as you increase your production. By adding together your fixed and variable costs at different levels of output, you can draw on a sheet of graph paper the relationship between total costs and output (see Figure 7a).

Figure 7. The break-even point

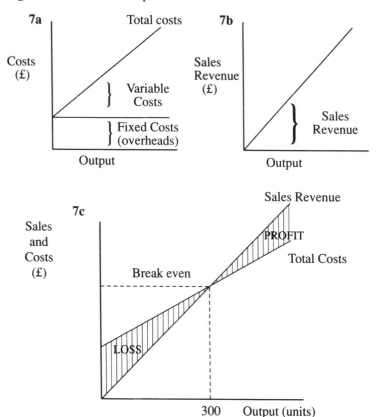

You can also chart very easily the relationship between output and sales revenue — you simply multiply the number of units sold by your average selling price per unit (see Figure 7b).

By superimposing the 'sales revenue' line on top of the 'total costs' line, you will be able to see clearly the level of output at which your revenue will be just enough to cover your costs — your 'break-even' point. The firm shown in Figure 7c will need to produce and sell 300 units in order to break even. If they sell less than 300 units, they will make a loss, since total costs will be greater than total revenue. If they sell more than 300 units, they will make a profit.

It is really quite straightforward to apply the same technique to your own operation. Provided you have drawn the graph accurately (and have done your sums correctly in the first place), you will be able to read off the amount of profit or loss likely to arise at different levels of output and sales. It almost goes without saying that this basic information is vital if you are to have effective control of what you are doing.

The contribution

There is an alternative way of looking at this problem. It begins by accepting that within a given scale of operations (i.e. with your existing plant, machinery and workforce), your overheads are more or less fixed and do not change as output is increased or reduced. Any attempt to allocate these overheads to different levels of output and between different products is bound to be wrong. Therefore, it is argued, a better way to proceed is to work out the 'gross margin' on each product and, where necessary, on each large order. The gross margin is simply the difference between the selling price and total direct costs, ignoring indirect costs at this stage. This amount is what is available to contribute towards the payment of overheads and other indirect costs, and once these have been met in full, to profits. For obvious reasons, it is often referred to as 'the contribution'. An example is shown in Figure 8. The main advantage of this method is that it leaves you free to set the price at a level appropriate to market conditions. It is particularly useful in helping you to make the right decision in two specific situations:

- where your total production capacity is limited, and you have to decide how much of each different product you should make;
- where you have to decide whether a particular large order on special terms should be accepted or not.

Figure 8. Pricing based on 'the contributions'

	£	£
Sales revenue (500 units @ £12)		6,000
Less:		
Direct materials @ £5.00 per unit	2,500	
Direct labour @ £2.00 per unit	1,000	
Total direct costs		3,500
Gross margin (the contribution)		2,500
Gross margin per unit		5.00

Different products

In choosing between different products, you should give the greatest weight to those which make the greatest contribution. Obviously there are other factors which are also relevant to that decision, and it would be extremely unwise to concentrate your resources entirely on the single product which yields the highest contribution. We have already discussed the need to develop a balanced portfolio of products which will appeal to your target group of customers, as well as the risks of being a one-product company.

Individual orders

Focussing your attention on the contribution also makes it easier to decide whether or nor it is worthwhile accepting a particular order. This situation can arise as a result of negotiations with a large potential customer, where quite often you will find the outcome is that you can obtain a big order if you are prepared to offer special terms. As long as you are working at less than maximum capacity, you should consider accepting any additional business which makes a positive contribution to covering your overheads. Once you have reached the point where you are operating at more or less maximum capacity, you should accept only those orders which yield the highest contribution. If you are going through a very slack period, it may be worthwhile reducing your price to a level at which you are not actually making a profit on a particular order, but which still makes a contribution to meeting your overheads, which you will have to pay anyway regardless of your total output. Of course, this tactic should be used very infrequently — you will not last long if you apply it to all of your pricing decisions. You should remember that it is very difficult to raise your price again once you have conceded a reduction to a particular customer, and also that these things have a nasty habit of getting around fairly quickly — if you do a special deal for one customer, the others are likely to hear about it and demand the same treatment. The way around this is to work out in advance what sort of bulk purchase discounts you would be prepared to offer, following the general principle that the bigger the order, the bigger the discount you can afford simply because your overheads will be spread over a larger number of units of output.

The 'contribution' approach to pricing is widely practised today in large companies. There is no reason at all why smaller firms should not use it as well. In practice, it is a bit more complicated than the brief outline presented here, and you would be wise to consult your accountant before you try to apply it. It is also sound advice to continue with more traditional cost-plus methods at least while you are learning the ins and outs of the 'contribution' approach.

As a final word on the whole subject of pricing, just remember:

**IT IS THE MARKET WHICH DETERMINES
THE PRICE YOU CAN CHARGE.
YOUR COSTS MERELY DETERMINE
WHETHER OR NOT YOU WILL
MAKE A PROFIT AT THIS PRICE.**

Summary of Key Points
1. There is no such thing as 'the' one and only price for anything. For any good or service, there is a range of possible prices, and buyers and sellers are free to agree on a price within this range. Different versions of a particular product are offered by alternative suppliers at various prices. A single supplier often negotiates a different price with some customers for the same product.
2. Purchasing decisions are not made solely on the basis of price. People choose between the competing alternatives available to them on the basis of what they believe represents the best value for money. Their views on what is good value depend to some extent on how well off they are, and on the price of competitive products.
3. Price is often taken as an indicator of quality.
4. Some goods and services are very sensitive to price changes, in that a small rise in their price will result in a substantial drop in demand. Some other goods and services are relatively insensitive to price changes. It is worth giving some thought to how sensitive your particular products are to changes in their price.

Setting a Price

5. There are basically three pricing strategies you can choose. You can set your prices at a level which is lower than, about the same as or higher than most of your competition.
6. Adopting a low-price strategy is not usually a good idea for a small firm. This often implies operating at cost levels which are quite impossible to achieve on a small scale. Small firms which adopt a high volume/low profit margin strategy generally find it very difficult to survive in the longer term. They often fall victims to the extreme competitive pressure exerted by bigger companies operating at much higher levels of output.
7. A low volume/high mark-up strategy is often more likely to ensure the long-term survival of a small firm. But you can only charge a higher price by offering your customers something distinctively different and valuable to them. The difference may be a real technical advantage, better quality, better service or better presentation.
8. Many small firms set their prices simply by calculating their total costs and adding on a traditional profit margin; but this ignores market forces. A better approach is to focus on 'the contribution' to profits arising from each product and even each large order, if necessary. As an absolute minimum, your should know your 'break-even' level of sales and output.
9. The price you can charge is set by the market. Your costs merely determine whether or not you will make a profit at this price.

6.
Organising Distribution

Under the bonnet of your car, you will find a thing called the distributor. If this component is faulty, the car simply will not go — even though every other part is in perfect working order. The same is true of a company. You must make sure that whatever you are selling is made available to the people who ultimately buy and use it:
- in good condition
- at the time they need it
- at a location which is convenient for them.

This implies paying attention to the physical logistics of distribution in terms of packaging, transportation, storage and so on. But the first and most basic decision you need to make is whether to organise your distribution:
- direct to the customer, or
- through an intermediary or middleman.

In order to make that decision, you must go back to the absolute basics and ask yourself again some of the fundamental marketing questions:
- Who is my customer?
- Where, when, how and how often do they buy?

You will find that answering these basic questions will provide the answer to what kind of distribution system you need. As a very rough general rule, if a market is made up of a very large number of customers each buying relatively small amounts on a fairly regular basis, some kind of intermediary will almost certainly be required. If only a small number of customers is involved, direct distribution is feasible and the services of an intermediary may not be necessary. Quite often, the number of options is limited, and you will find yourself setting up the same kind of distribution system as everyone else. But do not simply copy what everyone else is doing without thinking about it. Devising a new and more effective method of distribution may well be the way to give you a competitive edge over the opposition. You should also bear in mind that the choice between direct distribution and using an inter-

Organising Distribution

mediary is not a simple black and white decision. It is often not a case of one method or the other. Frequently you will find that it makes good sense to use both approaches.

DISTRIBUTION DIRECT TO THE CUSTOMER
Advantages
The main reasons why it may be worthwhile to consider distributing your products direct to the customer rather than through an intermediary are:

- You retain the full profit margin and avoid having to sacrifice part of it to the middleman.
- You retain total control over how your product is handled and presented.
- You have a better opportunity to obtain feedback from the customer and to organise after-sales service.
- You can concentrate the sales effort on your products and avoid the risk of too much attention being given to other products.
- You may not be able to persuade intermediaries to stock your products.

The idea of being able to hold on to the full mark-up for yourself is superficially very attractive. In theory, you can then use the additional revenue you have earned to increase your profits, or alternatively you can become more competitive by lowering your price. But setting up your own direct distribution system can be expensive, and the resulting improvement in your profit margin may ultimately be more imaginary than real. Retaining full control over what happens to your product in transit and over how it is displayed are major advantages which are not easily overlooked, as are the other benefits listed above.

Disadvantages
However there are also major disadvantages associated with direct distribution. These include the following.

- You will incur substantial additional costs, no matter how efficient you are — and this money might well be used to greater advantage elsewhere in the business.
- You will incur a substantial additional burden in terms of management time and effort.
- You will have to acquire the specialised expertise needed to organise an effective system.
- You will severely limit the total number of customers you can service.

Alternatives

In many kinds of business, there is a direct link to a relatively small number of final customers, and there is no need for the intervention of an intermediary. The best examples of this are perhaps suppliers of machinery and industrial components of various kinds. In this situation, the distribution problem is often reduced to organising appropriate transportation. But as the business expands, it may be necessary to employ the services of some kind of third party as sales agent and/or distributor.

In consumer markets, direct sales and therefore direct distribution can be organised in many different ways, including:

- Setting up your own retail outlets
- Van sales
- Mail order
- 'Party plan' sales

Your own retail outlets

Setting up your own retail outlets does not necessarily imply a chain of permanent shops. This would obviously be very expensive and difficult to organise, although the 'factory shop' located on your own premises is a fairly easy option. It is possible to set up temporary outlets on an occasional basis — for example, by renting floor space in the entrance hall of a shopping centre for a couple of weekends. This is a useful way of getting started and can be quite effective in generating sales if you cover a number of centres over a wide geographical area in rotation. A stall at the many open-air street markets throughout the country is another alternative, but one which is not really all that attractive as a long term proposition.

Van sales

The idea of selling straight off the back of a van should not be dismissed too early. You probably have a mental image of a clapped-out and rather dirty vehicle crawling slowly around rural areas, selling the odd stone of potatoes and packet of washing powder. But remember that there are plenty of examples of substantial businesses which were built up on this very basic method of direct distribution — bread and milk, to name but two of them. A more up-to-date example is provided by a small firm which manufacturers specialist paints for vehicles and boats. A substantial proportion of its turnover is derived from the activities of van salesmen who tour the garages, repair shops and boatyards on a regular weekly or fortnightly schedule. It works well mainly because it suits the customers who want to avoid holding a large stock covering all the

Organising Distribution

different colour combinations required, who wish to buy relatively small quantities, and who find it difficult to predict their precise requirements in advance. It is also very cost-effective from the point of view of the manufacturer.

Mail order

Mail order originated as a means of supplying consumer goods to customers in remote areas of the United States. More recently in Britain and Ireland, mail order has acquired something of a reputation for being as much a way of obtaining goods on credit, rather than simply making them more available. No doubt you have come across a large and glossy sales catalogue prepared by one of the big mail order companies. This traditional kind of mail order business is operated on a very large scale, and it is not suggested as a feasible alternative method of distribution for the smaller firm. However many small firms have developed very successful variations on the mail order theme. One approach is the specialist catalogue concentrating on a fairly narrow product range, and offering a wider and more esoteric selection than is normally available in the shops. Seed catalogues provide a good example of how this type of distribution works. A basic requirement is to produce a good-quality, attractive catalogue — duplicated lists are not usually very successful. The availability of the catalogue is made known to prospective consumers by means of small display advertisements in appropriate specialist magazines. To avoid the problem of non-payment, 'cash with order' is often required, but to allay the natural caution of the average customer, a 'money back if not satisfied' guarantee is also included.

An alternative type of mail order is where customers respond directly to a newspaper, magazine or television advertisement. This method has been around for a very long time, but has recently been given something of a new lease of life by companies prepared to use it on a large scale — for example to market records and tapes. At that level it can be a very risky undertaking, mainly due to the very heavy advertising costs involved. But on a more limited scale, it is another option worth considering for some types of business.

Yet another type of mail order is based on sending out leaflets to a selected mailing list of possible customers inviting them to 'complete and return the attached order form'. This is being used successfully to market books, clothing and even fitted kitchens and bedrooms. One of the keys to success is the quality and accuracy of the mailing list, and there are firms which specialise in supplying lists of various kinds. There are also specialist agencies who are prepared to handle the printing, addressing and mailing aspects of the operation, including the use of modern technology, so that every potential customer receives a personalised letter. There is, of course, no reason why a small firm should not compile its own mailing lists using the telephone book and other directories, together with its own records of existing and former customers and enquirers.

Mail order is obviously only feasible for products which are relatively lightweight, small in size and durable enough to be sent by post. It also helps if they look good in a photograph, can be described in terms which are attractive, and are not generally available elsewhere. Standard widely-available products can usually be sold by mail order only at a very substantially reduced price. Mail order is a specialised operation in itself, and you should think through very carefully all the issues involved before you decide to try it.

Party plan

'Party plan' sales and distribution is widely used for some kinds of children's and women's clothing, for cosmetics, and for those famous plastic storage containers and kitchen utensils (Tupperware). It requires tight control over a large number of more-or-less amateur sales people and takes a lot of organisation to generate a reasonable sales volume. Nevertheless it is an alternative you might consider.

DISTRIBUTION THROUGH AN INTERMEDIARY
Advantages

There are a number of substantial advantages to be derived from using a middleman to distribute your products. These include:

- increasing substantially the number of potential customers presented with an opportunity to buy your products;
- carrying out some major tasks which you would otherwise have to do yourself;
- sharing some of the marketing costs needed to maximise your sales;
- providing specialised expertise which you may not possess.

Selling through a nationwide retail chain is possibly the best example of how an intermediary can offer a consumer product to a far larger number of potential customers than a small manufacturer could ever hope to reach using direct distribution. But the same principle applies to industrial products — appointing a number of distributors in different parts of the country can increase significantly the size of the market in which

you are operating. The tasks which a middleman can undertake on your behalf include:
- storage/stock-holding
- sales promotion and merchandising
- selling
- providing credit facilities
- stocking spare parts/providing after-sales service
- delivery and installation

Not all of these functions are appropriate in every case, nor indeed is it guaranteed that the distributor will share marketing costs with you. However co-operative advertising and sales promotional activities are quite common and are a useful way of making a much bigger impact than you could possibly fund out of our own resources. Finally, retailing and other forms of distribution are in themselves highly specialised business activities requiring considerable expertise which most small firms cannot hope to match.

Disadvantages

There are also some disadvantages which arise as a result of channeling your goods through an intermediary. These include:
- a reduction of your profit margin and/or an increase in the selling price to the end-user;
- the risk that the middleman will end up controlling you, rather than the other way round;
- the risk that your product will not be given the attention it needs if it is to sell well.

Lost profits

Middlemen, of course, are not in business just for the fun of it — they are there to make money. It is therefore not unreasonable that they should seek to cover their costs and maximise the return on their investment. You may well be appalled to find that your product is being sold to the end-user at more or less twice the price the middleman paid you for it, but you have to take into account what it would cost you to set up your own distribution system, and what else you could do with the capital that would be tied up in it. To put it into perspective, how much do you think it would cost the Ford Motor Company to set up a world-wide dealer network from scratch? It would have to purchase sites, build and equip showrooms and servicing facilities, recruit and train staff, provide stocks, and manage the day-to-day running of all of them. The investment required would be enormous, and quite possibly beyond the reach of even a major multinational like Ford. You can easily see why it makes sense for the car manufacturers to arrange their distribution in the way they do. The same reasoning applies to your own situation, although obviously on a much smaller scale. It usually makes sense to forfeit some of your potential gross margin to have the benefit of the services which middlemen provide. The other possibility — that your products will be priced out of the market by an excessive mark-up added by your distributors — should also be considered against the background that they need sales just as much as you do. Most middlemen are very astute at judging what the market will bear. They will try to pressurise you into accepting as low a price as possible, but at the end of the day they have no reason to force you out of business by forcing you to accept a price you simply cannot meet. Of course, if your costs and in consequence your selling price are way out of line with competing products of similar quality, that is an altogether different problem not directly related to the distributor's mark-up.

Loss of independence
It can happen that a small firm becomes dependent on a single distributor for such a high proportion of its total sales that it is in effect controlled by the distributor. This situation seems to arise more often in consumer rather than industrial markets — for example where a large multiple retail chain takes most of the output of, say, a small food processing firm. It is not at all unusual for a small firm in this position to find that it is invited to market its product under the retailer's brand name. This will involve tightening still further the degree of control exercised by the retailer, who is very likely to insist on specifying the composition and ingredients of the product in detail, the packaging, how it is presented and so on. It may also mean agreeing to regular inspections of your premises to satisfy the retailer that you are meeting an acceptable level of hygiene, following the agreed production method and achieving required levels of output. You may also be required to deliver to locations and times specified by the retailer. An agreement of this kind is not necessarily a bad thing. It virtually guarantees you a certain level of sales, provided you can maintain the required standard. It greatly simplifies your marketing, which is reduced to a question of ensuring that you deliver the product as specified and on time.

There are, however, disadvantages inherent in 'own label' production. Your profit margin will be squeezed to the limit, but the horror stories you may have heard from time to time about small firms being exploited by the large retail chains are, generally speaking, quite untrue.

For the reasons noted above, it is not in the retailer's long-term interest to force you out of business. He or she will, of course, drive a hard bargain, but they realise that you are also in business to make a profit. There are many examples of small firms which have survived and prospered on the basis of a long-term relationship with a multiple retailer. The biggest single disadvantage, of course, is that you are very much at the mercy of your single customer. If you are approached with a 'retailer's own label' proposal, it is usually a more sensible strategy to insist that you retain the right to produce and market a version of the product under your own brand name. This will give you the capability of developing sales to other customers, thereby reducing your total dependence on a single outlet for your products.

Lack of attention
Using any kind of middleman for your distribution also incurs the risk that your product will not be given the attention it needs if it is to sell well. The great majority of middlemen handle a wide range of different products from different manufacturers, and there is always the possibility that your product will be lost somewhere in the crowd. There are two ways avoiding this problem. You can make a deliberate decision to link up with a small-scale distributor to whom your product is of major importance. The other alternative is to maintain regular and frequent contact with your distributor to make sure that your product is being pushed on through the distribution chain to the final customer in the volume needed to achieve your profit target.

TYPES OF INTERMEDIARY
There is an enormously wide variety of different types of middlemen currently operating in Ireland. To make some sense of the huge range of alternatives available, it is convenient to look at them under four broad headings:
- Retailers
- Wholesalers/merchants
- Distributors
- Agents

Retailers
Retailing is one of the most dynamic sectors of the economy, and there have been enormous changes in retailing methods and structures over recent years. These changes reflect broad social trends, in that the great majority of consumers have become more mobile, more affluent and

more sophisticated in expressing their wants and needs. Compared with even ten years ago, virtually every town of any size throughout Ireland has its own shopping centre which includes at least one of the major grocery retailers, together with a range of independently-owned smaller shops. In the bigger cities, suburban shopping centres have siphoned off at least some of the trade which was traditionally concentrated in the city centre. More recently, city centre traders have begun to fight back with the re-furbishment of older types of outlet and the building of new ones, often as part of a wider urban re-development scheme. Totally new types of retail outlets have been devised, so that the term 'retailers' now includes:

- multiple chain stores
- department stores
- DIY superstores
- discount warehouses
- garden centres
- boutiques/specialist shops
- voluntary chains
- traditional street-corner shops
- petrol stations
- franchised outlets

The multiples

It is no exaggeration to say that retailing in Ireland, both North and South, is dominated by a relatively few major multiples. This is most apparent in the grocery trade, where companies such as Dunnes Stores and Quinnsworth in the South and Stewarts, Crazy Prices and Wellworths in the North between them account for a very high proportion of total sales in this sector. The importance of that fact for the small manufacturer should not be overlooked. In one sense, there are literally millions of customers for food products. But in another sense, the total number of potential customers can be counted of the fingers of both hands. This only very slightly overstates the case, because to achieve any meaningful sales volume, you really need to go through the multiples.

The basic trading stance of the multiples depends on high volume combined with low profit margins, and they are very demanding indeed in their requirements. You will almost certainly have to be able to guarantee regular and frequent deliveries to individual outlets, or possibly to regional distribution centres. You may well be required to undertake the merchandising of your own products. In other words, you will have to assume responsibility for making sure that adequate supplies of your product are in the stores at the times required, and in some cases even to stack the products on the shelves. You will have to agree to participate from time to time in special promotions often involving a temporary price reduction, and you may well have to accept 'over-riders' on the basic price you have agreed — in other words, an additional bulk purchase discount if total sales in a given period exceed an agreed level. If you are thinking that all of this is not fair, and that these demands are unreasonable, you will just have to grin and bear it. The fact of the matter is that they hold the power, and they call the shots.

Most of the multiples which originally started out in the grocery trade have now diversified into a wide range of other goods — clothing and footwear, hardware, electrical goods and so on. Multiples are of course also prominent in many sectors other than groceries, and the situation is further complicated by the arrival of some of the major British retail chains onto the Irish scene (e.g. Marks and Spencers and BHS). Some of the Irish multiples (e.g. Dunnes Stores) operate on an all-Ireland basis, and it is a fairly safe bet that this will become a more prominent feature of retail trading in Ireland when the Single European Market is completed in 1992.

Department stores

Many of the traditional city-centre department stores ceased trading in the 1970s, forced out of business by the onslaught of the multiples. Those that have survived have done so essentially by going up-market. They depend for their custom on a reputation for providing high-quality goods and a pleasant environment in which to shop. They also continue to provide some of the additional features which have to some extent gone by the board in the high-volume multiple outlets — personalised service to the customer, 'free' delivery, and other services such as carpet fitting, or making-up curtains to the customer's individual specification.

The very name 'department' store gives you a clue to its basic organisational structure. Each department operates as a separate cost-centre and specialises in the purchase and resale of a particular range of goods. The key figure is the buyer, who decides well in advance what the department will offer and chooses the appropriate supplier. You should bear in mind that the lead times involved can be quite considerable, often up to a year in advance. For example, decisions are made and orders placed for the Christmas toy trade no later than the end of March each year.

One specific way of linking in with the department stores which you should be aware of is the possibility of opening a 'store within a store'.

This can work in a number of ways, but most typically it involves renting floor-space within the store to enable you to set up your own sales operation. Detailed negotiation is required on such matters as staffing — for instance whether you hire the services of an existing sales assistant or whether you provide your own — and on whether or not you will also be required to pay a commission on sales.

DIY superstores

DIY superstores, discount warehouses and garden centres are examples of more recently introduced forms of retailing. The way in which they operate illustrates the growing complexity of the retail scene. Many DIY superstores have diversified into furniture, household furnishings and gardening equipment. Some garden centres are also beginning to stock a wider range of leisure goods. Many discount warehouses, originally conceived as no frills, low-cost facilities most often specialising in electrical goods, furniture or carpets, are now improving their premises and moving slowly up-market. Here again, the basic trading stance is based on bulk purchasing at minimum price levels and subsequently high volume/low margin resale.

Specialist boutiques

The highly-specialised fashion boutique has been around for a long time, but a more recent phenomenon has been the emergence of specialist retailers trading is essentially the same way in respect of other types of goods. Typically, these tend to be small-scale, low volume, high mark-up operations depending for their survival on the growing consumer demand for exclusive and unique high-quality products. These features in fact make them a very attractive proposition for the smaller manufacturer, with less pressure on margins and much lower volumes to contend with. However, as a general rule, they will only handle products which are distinctively different in some way.

Voluntary chains

The voluntary chains of independent retailers (such as Spar, Mace, VG) were formed originally by food wholesalers who saw their traditional role being decimated by the advent of the multiples. They responded by persuading small independent retailers, who were also facing the same threat, to trade solely with them. In return for agreeing to take the bulk of their supplies from the wholesaler, the independent retailers were provided with a common identity which enabled them to be advertised through the mass media, with 'own label' brands, and advice on merchandising, stock control and accounting systems. This approach has enabled both parties to the agreement to survive. Central buying enables the small trader to derive some of the benefits of bulk purchasing, and thus remain more or less competitive on price with the supermarkets run by the multiples. The convenience to customers arising from their late opening hours and street-corner location also helps.

These advantages also largely explain the continued survival of the many small independent street-corner shops which are still very much part of the retail scene. Their functions are now being taken over in some areas by shops operated in conjunction with petrol filling stations — the modern version of the street-corner shop. These types of outlets obtain their supplies either from 'cash and carry' wholesalers, and by means of regular orders obtained from a van salesman, or through a sales representative who calls frequently to confirm repeat orders of standard items.

Franchising

It is estimated that there are now more than sixty different retail franchise ventures operating in Ireland. These include some very well-known names—MacDonald's, Pizzaland, Benetton, The Body Shop and Prontaprint. The basic method of operation is that the person operating the franchise buys a standardised business format and subsequently pays a commission on sales to the franchise owner. There is usually no opportunity for you to sell your products to a franchise operator, since the details of what can and cannot be sold are specified in the franchise agreement. However setting up your own franchise operation is a method of distribution which may well be worth considering in certain circumstances.

Wholesalers

A wholesaler may be defined as a company which buys in bulk the products of a number of different manufacturers and resells them, usually in smaller quantities. The key point as far as you are concerned is that a wholesaler is a customer who buys, takes legal title to and accepts delivery of your products; whether or not he or she can resell them is his/her problem, not yours — but of course if he/she has any difficulty in selling them, your chances of obtaining repeat orders are fairly slim, to put it mildly.

Most wholesalers focus their activities on a specific industrial sector — e.g. engineering, or the building trade, or clothing — and see themselves as being primarily in the business of meeting the needs of their own customers with whom they have had a long-standing relation-

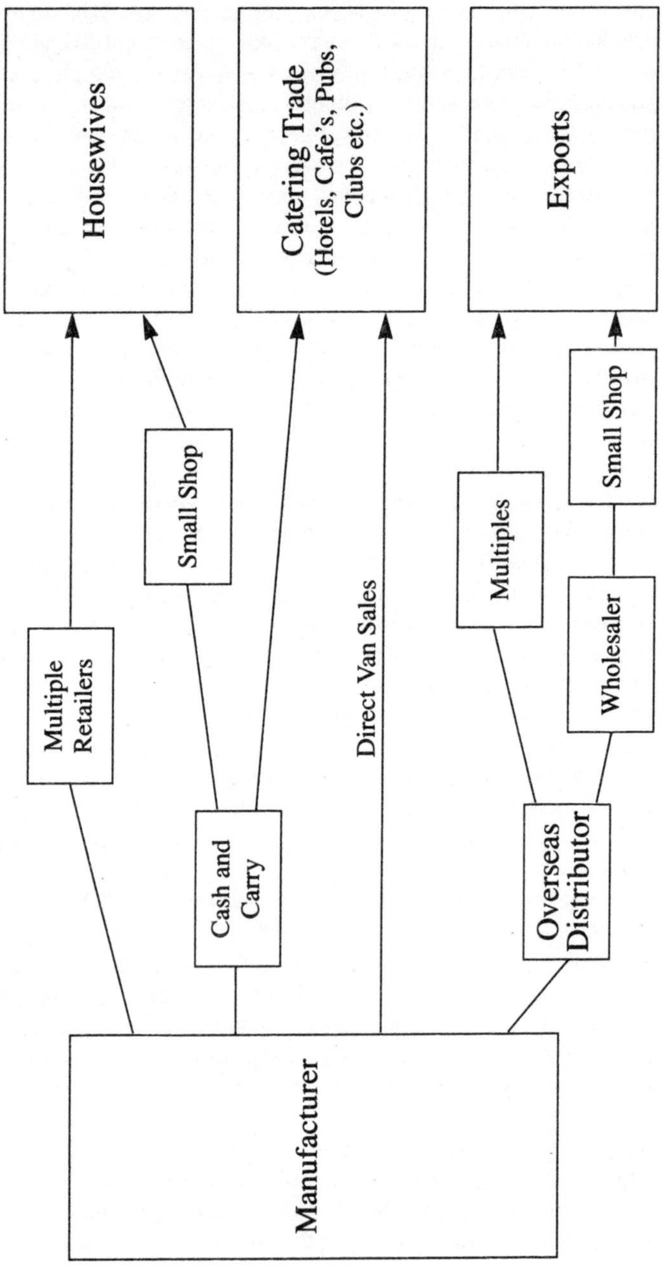

Figure 9. Organising Distribution (a standard food product)

ship. They see it as their job to be able to provide whatever is required either from stock or at very short notice; they do not usually see themselves as having a responsibility to push the products of one particular manufacturer as opposed to another. Generally speaking, they are only prepared to deal with established manufacturers who are well-known to their own customers. For that reason, small manufacturers often find it difficult to persuade a wholesaler to stock their products, and are often disappointed with the resulting sales volume if and when they succeed in doing so. The only way round these problems is persistence and persuasion — do not take an initial brush-off as the final outcome of your approach — but it helps a lot if you can mention that you are already supplying one or two major customers. Once they have agreed to handle your product, it is essential that you maintain contact to ensure that they make some kind of sales push. In this context, the offer of a slightly higher margin than other manufacturers often helps.

Cash-and-carry
The cash-and-carry warehouse providing a wide range of goods to small independent retailers is a relatively recent innovation in wholesaling which has expanded dramatically in recent years. There is now a network covering virtually the whole of Ireland, with some companies operating both North and South (e.g. Musgraves), although many of the smaller cash-and-carry outlets in rural areas are totally independent. The great majority of cash-and-carry wholesalers sell only to bona fide traders, but it is a reflection of the intensifying pressure in the distributive industry that some of them have relaxed their rules to such an extent that it is very easy indeed for a member of the general public to obtain a card by registering as a customer, thus enabling them to buy direct at wholesale prices rather than through a conventional retailer.

Distributors
There is really very little difference between a wholesaler and a distributor in terms of their basic trading practices and legal status. However the term 'distributor' is generally used to denote an intermediary who is prepared to accept a specific commitment to sell your products and not those of your competitors.

Agents
The key distinction between a sales agent and a distributor or wholesaler is that agents do not actually buy the product from you — they take orders and pass them on to you; you then invoice the customer

directly. The agent earns a living by being paid a commission on each sale, which can vary between seven and twenty per cent or more of the total value of the order. The main advantage of using sales agents is that they are not employees, but are in business on their own account. Thus you incur costs only on the sales they generate, and you can make a substantial saving on overheads — agents are responsible for providing their own car, office, possibly a showroom and so on. The main disadvantage is that most agents handle a range of products, and there is always the risk that your product will not be given enough attention. One way of minimising the risk is to insist that an agent acting for you does not also have any directly competing products in his or her portfolio. Another approach is to choose an agent who has a fairly limited range of products, and for whom sales of your product would be important in terms of his/her overall commission earnings.

Problems with agents
There are two main problems involved in selling and distributing through agents or distributors:
- finding a good one
- controlling their activities

Most people with experience of running a small business will tell you that it is easy enough to find an agent or distributor — the problem is finding a good one! You will often see advertisements placed in trade journals by agents and distributors looking for new products. The big worry with these, of course, is the sneaking suspicion that if they were any good, they would not need to advertise. You can place an advertisement yourself, but you need to be very careful indeed in checking out the replies you receive — it is a safe bet that you will get at least one who is a little bit suspect. You can sometimes identify possible agents or distributors by attending trade fairs and exhibitions. But perhaps the most effective approach is to do a bit of basic research in the particular territory you wish the agent to service for you. Who handles your competitors' products? Who deals with the sort of customers you are likely to want but does not have a product similar to yours in their current range? This kind of information can be obtained by simply asking round. Contact the local Chamber of Commerce; ask buyers in big firms and/or retail outlets; ask other business people you know in the area.

Do not be surprised if you encounter a couple of false starts. It is entirely typical to discover that contacts who seem to meet all your requirements turn out to have feet of clay when you check them out in detail. This can also be done informally by talking to people. But before entering into a formal agreement, it is essential that you obtain a bank reference.

Agency agreements
When you have identified someone with whom you can do business, you need to formalise your arrangements by entering into a written agreement which will be the basis for your future relationship. Such an agreement should specify:
- the products to be sold
- the rate of commission payable and how it is to be paid
- the territory to be covered
- procedures for transmitting orders to you
- the duration of the agreement

You may feel that this is going a bit far, but the bitter experience of many small firms over the years suggests that is is simply not enough to rely on a 'gentleman's agreement' arrived at by shaking hands at the end of a good lunch. Differences of opinion may arise, and the best way to avoid them is for each party to be absolutely clear from the outset about what is involved. The other way in which you can control the activities of agents or distributors is by keeping in touch with them on a regular basis. It is not enough to sign the agreement and then sit back and wait for things to happen.

Franchising
An alternative method of distributing your product or service is by entering into franchise agreements. The main advantages of this approach is that it enables you to expand your business fairly rapidly with minimal capital outlay, and without encountering the day-to-day problems associated with running your own outlets. A further advantage is that your franchise operators are likely to be more strongly motivated than salaried employees to making the venture a success. However to run your business on a franchising basis, you need to develop a 'business format' which is:
- distinctive in its range and/or its business approach;
- capable of earning a profit margin big enough to give a return both to you and to the franchise operator;
- capable of being re-produced successfully by others.

The 'business format' needs to have been developed and refined over a reasonable period of time before you can begin to think of offering it to others on a franchise basis. As well as the basic product, it also usually includes arrangements for training, promotional support and sales methods. Revenue is generated by requiring the franchise operator to pay you an initial fee plus ongoing royalties in proportion to sales. There may also be an advertising and promotional support levy, and the normal mark-up on goods or equipment which you supply. The contract setting out the terms of the agreement should include a precise definition of the franchise operator's rights and duties, including:

- the type of business and the uses which can be made of the business name;
- the geographical area and the types of customers covered by the franchise;
- the initial payment, subsequent royalties and any other payments required;
- the length of time for which the franchise will run, and the rights of both parties to extend or renew the contract beyond its original term;
- the terms and conditions under which the contract may be terminated;
- the rights of the operator to sell the franchise to a third party.

The above is only a very brief outline of what is involved in franchising. It is essential that you consider very carefully all the different aspects of this form of trading, taking legal advice if you decide to proceed down this road.

PHYSICAL DISTRIBUTION

Managing the physical logistics of distribution is a very wide area in its own right which requires careful advance planning. It includes making appropriate arrangements in three key areas:

- packaging
- stock-holding
- transportation

Packaging

In consumer markets, your packaging has an important role to play in selling your products. It helps to create an overall image and to establish the difference between your products and those of your competitors. But do not forget that, as well as the wrapper or pack which is bought by the final customer, you will also have to provide secondary packaging to protect the product during transportation and storage. Your packaging must be durable enough to cope with a wide range of potential hazards, including:

- damage by mechanical handling;
- product loss due to evaporation or leakages;
- contamination by dust, dirt, insects and rodents
- chemical change due to extreme fluctuations in temperature, moisture gain or loss;
- theft.

It must also be convenient to use in terms of storage, stacking and opening, and where possible designed to minimise transport costs. There has been a revolution in the technology of packaging materials in recent years, with new materials (e.g. polystyrene, polyethylene film) and handling techniques (e.g. containerisation) being introduced. Fortunately there is plenty of expertise available from printers and suppliers of packaging materials to provide sound advice on these matters.

Stock-holding

Holding stocks of finished goods costs you a lot of money which you could put to good use elsewhere in the business. The main cost elements involved are:

- the wages of staff employed in this area;
- heat, light and insurance;
- additional measures to avoid deterioration/spoilage of the product (e.g. chilled cabinets);
- loss of interest on capital tied up.

Unfortunately it is virtually impossible to organise things in such a way that no stocks need to be held. The difficulty is that, to be efficient, you need to produce at a fairly constant rate, but the pattern of demand from customers tends to fluctuate up and down according to their circumstances. Sometimes these fluctuations can be predicted quite easily — for example, where there are obvious seasonal peaks and troughs in demand — and due allowance made in your production schedule. There are also circumstances where it makes sense to increase your production and build up your stocks — for example, when you anticipate a substantial increase in the cost of your materials. However most of the time, the challenge is to maintain your stocks at a level which both:

- minimises your costs as far as possible; and
- provides the customers with a satisfactory level of service.

It costs you money every time you lose an order because a certain item is out of stock, and the loss can be much greater than the value of the order — a customer may well lose patience, go to one of your competitors, and stay there. The only certain way to avoid this possibility is to maintain very high stocks — but that costs you money in other ways. What you need to do is to establish the optimum service level.

The optimum service level may be measured in a number of different ways, but perhaps the simplest is to express it as follows:

$$\text{CUSTOMER SERVICE LEVEL} = \left(\frac{\text{NO. OF TIMES AN ORDER CAN BE MET}}{\text{NO. OF TIMES AN ORDER IS PLACED}}\right)\%$$

A specific example may help to clarify this. Assume that over a given period (say a month), a total of fifty orders for a particular product is received, but that on ten occasions the order could not be supplied from stock. The customer service level is calculated as:

$$\left(\frac{40}{50}\right)\% = \frac{40}{50} \times \frac{100}{1} = 80\%$$

Without going into detail, it is widely accepted that stock-holding costs begin to increase substantially as customer service levels rise above eighty per cent. Conversely, customer satisfaction levels begin to fall off sharply if you fall much below eighty per cent. It is not suggested that eighty per cent is the appropriate customer service level for every firm in every kind of industry — but it is a useful rough guideline to work to. You will need to work out your own optimum level on the basis of your own experience of inventory costs and customer service requirements.

Transportation

You will obviously need some kind of transportation to run your business efficiently, even if it is only a fairly elderly van. But as the business expands, you will need to decide at some stage whether to continue using your own transport to distribute your products or to sub-contract this to someone else. The advantages of developing your own fleet of vehicles include:

- maintaining more effective control over product handling and delivery times;
- creating an image of 'bigness' by having your company name appearing frequently in the traffic.

The disadvantages are primarily:

- the capital tied up in vehicles (although leasing and contract hire are less expensive alternatives);
- the substantial running costs involved — labour, fuel, maintenance;

Organising Distribution 97

- the additional demands on limited management time and expertise.

There are plenty of examples of smaller firms which operate their own transport, but these tend to be in situations involving short, frequent journeys using well-established routes — e.g. a bakery delivering to retail outlets. Where distribution requires long-haul journeys or specialised transport (e.g. temperature controlled), it is much more common to sub-contract the task to the transport professionals.

Transportation also needs to be considered as another aspect of optimising customer service levels. It is important that you should find out your customers' expectations in terms of delivery. You are unlikely to obtain many repeat orders if you take ten days to deliver when all your competitors normally take no more than two or three. Conversely, there is not much point in your incurring the higher costs likely to be involved in guaranteeing delivery within two days if customers are quite happy with ten. You need to strike an appropriate balance between:

- the risk of losing sales because your delivery times are too long; and
- the higher costs of guaranteeing rapid delivery.

Unfortunately there is no hard and fast answer which can be easily applied to every firm; this is another situation which is specific to your own operation. You will need to work out the right answer for your own case, but it is better to do so on the basis of a little bit of advance research rather than by trial and error. The errors may prove to be very expensive.

Summary of Key Points

1. An efficient distribution system is essential to make sure that your product is made available to your customers in good condition, at the time they need it, and at a location which is convenient for them.
2. A large number of alternative methods of distribution are available. In choosing which is the best for your company, you need to go right back to the basics of where, when, how and how often your customers buy your products.
3. Distribution direct to the customer has a number of advantages — you retain the full profit margin and total control over how your product is handled. Its main disadvantages are the substantial additional costs involved and the additional management time and effort needed to organise it.
4. Distribution through an intermediary greatly increases the number of customers serviced and is usually more efficient and less

expensive than direct distribution. However, some reduction in your profit margin is inevitable, and there is always the risk that the middleman will end up controlling you.
5. There is an enormously wide variety of different types of middlemen currently operating in Ireland, including retailers, wholesalers, merchants, distributors and agents. Even within the retail sector there are many different types of outlet, ranging from nationwide multiples to the independent street-corner shop.
6. Consumer products are mostly distributed through retailers and cash-and-carry wholesalers. Industrial products are usually distributed through specialist wholesalers or merchants.
7. Many small firms employ the services of an independent agent to obtain orders for them. This approach reduces their selling costs substantially, since they pay commission only on sales generated. The problems are in finding a good agent and keeping effective control of his or her activities.
8. The physical logistics of distribution — packaging, stock-holding and transportation — require careful advance planning. Packaging has an important promotional role to play, as well as providing protection for the product. Holding stocks of finished goods is very expensive, and it is essential to calculate the lowest level of stocks you can hold, consistent with maintaining a satisfactory level of service to your customers.

A Case History
Twenty years ago, the distribution system employed by a small firm which manufacturers a range of added-value chicken-based products was very simple indeed. A fleet of vans was filled up at the factory every morning and toured the area, following a set route and calling at shops twice a week. The distribution arrangements in place are now much more complex. (See Figure 9.)

The company basically services three market segments — housewives, the catering trade and the export market. To meet the need of the housewife, the product is channelled in bulk to regional depots maintained by the multiples and symbol group retailers, from whence it is dispatched as required to individual outlets throughout the country. At least one multiple now requires delivery direct from the factory to their local branches, using sophisticated modern computer technology to place orders and record transactions. The product is also sold in bulk to cash-and-carry wholesalers who sell it onwards to small shopkeepers, publicans and other independent traders. Much of the catering trade is in fact still serviced by direct van sales, although some of their requirements are supplied through specialist suppliers or cash-and-carry wholesalers.

Export business to England is handled by a distributor who has a large depot near Manchester. A refrigerated container leaves the factory every other night, arriving there early the next morning.

Because the product is perishable and involves handling a large number of small items, maintaining efficient distribution arrangements is a key management task for this particular company.

7.
Contacting the Customer

Is every potential customer aware of your existence and of what you have to offer? If not, what are you going to do about it? You should ask yourself these two questions and think carefully before you answer them. They are absolutely fundamental to your success or failure. If most of the people who are likely to buy whatever it is you want to sell to them have never even heard of you, then your chances of staying in business are fairly remote. Even if you can be reasonably confident that a sufficient number of them have at least heard of you, you also need to ask yourself what they think of you. Have you a good reputation, or not? Before you go any further you need to be very clear about:

- Who *exactly* you need to contact
- What you need to say to them
- How you are going to do it
- How much you are going to spend

WHOM DO YOU NEED TO CONTACT?

The obvious answer is that you need to contact everyone who might become a customer, but you need to be a bit more precise that that. On the one hand, you run the risk of losing valuable business if somehow or other you miss out an important group of potential buyers. The other side of the coin is that you can waste a lot of money by defining your target audience too widely so that you end up contacting people who are never going to buy anything from you. You need to make sure that you avoid both of these traps. Consider for a moment the simple example of someone running a hairdressing business located, say, in the city of Cork. A lot of business could be lost by concentrating solely on women, ignoring the fact that many men also regularly need the services of a hairdresser. Conversely, a lot of money could be wasted by advertising in a national as opposed to a local newspaper. It is, after all, highly unlikely that anybody living in Belfast or Dublin would travel to Cork just for a haircut (although it might be worthwhile contacting people staying in the local hotels).

Another point worth remembering is that quite often you need to contact not only the actual buyer but also the people who influence the buying decision. This is particularly important if you are selling to other companies or big organisations. For example, the decision to buy a new piece of machinery will be taken by the Managing Director, but almost certainly he or she will take the advice of the Production Manager before he/she makes up his or her mind and chooses one of the various alternatives available. The same principle applies to many consumer products. If you are trying to sell a new bicycle to ten-year-olds, you will not only have to persuade them that this is the very model they have been looking for; you will also have to convince their parents that it is safe and well enough made to stand up to the punishment the child will inflict on it.

Your target audience
The importance of researching and defining precisely the various subgroups which comprise your target market was emphasised in Chapter 2. One of the major reasons for doing so was to enable you to make sensible decisions about whom you need to contact. If you have done your basic research, you should be able to write down a brief description of what is referred to in marketing jargon as your 'target audience'. Who *exactly* are they? If you are selling a consumer product or service, try to define your target audience in terms of their age, sex, marital status, social class and area of residence (e.g 'middle-class married women over thirty years of age living in Greater Dublin').

If you are selling to other companies, see if you can come up with a clear description of your prospective customers which includes their job-title, the industrial/commercial sector in which they operate, and their geographical location (e.g 'creamery managers in the South-west region'). It is quite possible that in doing this, you will need to define several distinctly different groups of people; but this is by no means a problem. On the contrary, it is a major advantage in refining your overall marketing strategy because you will then be able to identify more clearly what you need to say to each sub-group. The chances are you will decide that you need to convey a rather different message to each of them. You will also be in a much better position to rank them in order of priority, and decide which is your primary (most important) target market, which is the second most important, and so on. This will help you to make decisions about how to allocate to maximum effect the limited amount of money you can afford to spend on contacting the customer. Defining your target audience as precisely as you possibly can is the essential first step in planning your whole approach.

WHAT DO YOU NEED TO TELL THEM?

The overall message you need to communicate to potential customers is a little bit more complicated than simply saying: 'Here I am — buy from me'. You need to tell them what they can buy from you and give them some reasons why they should do so. You need to build up a good image so that the name of your company and/or your products is immediately recognised by people living in the area you service. In other words, the message you should aim at getting across includes three different elements:
- providing information
- persuasion
- developing a good reputation

Information

As an absolute basic minimum, potential customers need to know the name of your company, its address, and its telephone number. If you sell mostly to other companies, your FAX number is also necessary in this day and age. You may well be thinking that this is so obvious that it is an insult to your intelligence — but many small firms manage to get it wrong, believe it or not. An engineering company recently spent £5000 on a very attractive brochure which included photographs of the Managing Director and the Sales Manager, but did not give its phone number. The whole effect is spoiled by the little bits of paper which have to be stuck into each brochure to provide this vital piece of basic information. A car distributor in Belfast regularly advertises in the local evening paper with some very attractive offers, but the advertisements do not give his address (honestly!) To be fair, he gives the name of the little side-street where his showroom is to be found, but does not tell us what part of the city it is in. He assumes most people know. He probably loses quite a lot of business because many of them don't, and it is much easier for them to go on to the next advertisement rather than make an effort to find out where he is.

Again, it is fairly obvious that potential customers need information about the products and services you provide, but you should think carefully about how much detail is required. In the early stage, when your objective is simply to let them know of your existence, it may be enough to describe your product range in broad terms. The technical details quite often can be left until later and given only to serious enquirers who have contacted you as a result of your previous efforts.

From time to time, you will also need to communicate information about a specific event — e.g. a special offer available for a limited period, or the launch of a new product.

Persuasion

The first step in contacting potential customers is to make sure that they know who you are, what you offer, and where to find you. The next step is to persuade them to think seriously about giving you an order. To do this, you need to communicate to them the benefits of your particular product or service, compared with other competing alternatives. This is not as easy as it sounds. There may in fact be little or no obvious difference between what you and your competitors provide. You need to try and think in the same way as a potential customer, and tease out what he or she is most concerned with. You may have to phrase complicated technical advantages in a way which people can understand. You may find it more useful to concentrate on the service you provide rather than on the product itself, giving emphasis perhaps to speed of delivery or a guarantee of good workmanship in installation and servicing. In the case of consumer of products, you may need to draw their attention to less-tangible benefits, such as the fact that your product is 'healthy' or 'natural'. You will certainly have to establish your credibility as a potential supplier — people must believe that you can and will provide what you are claiming. Many small firms have found that the first hurdle they have to get over is to convince buyers that they are reputable and reliable, because buyers will simply not place an order until they have reached that point of trust.

Reputation

Most big companies have a well-established corporate image built up at substantial cost and over many years. Many of their products are internationally-known household names. It is totally unrealistic for a small firm to even think of achieving the level of immediate public recognition enjoyed by the major multinationals. Just to put it into perspective, at a recent conference organised by the Irish Management Institute, Tony O'Reilly of Heinz claimed that to achieve national consumer recognition in the USA for a previously unknown product, a company would require an outlay of about $100 million over a five-to-seven year period. It is very easy, and not unknown, for a firm to spend £1 million on launching a new consumer product on the Irish market. This level of marketing expenditure is clearly way beyond the reach of the average small business. But it is essential to aim at building up a good reputation and becoming well-known within the limited locality in which you operate.

Of course you will not be able to do all of this all at once. To achieve any worthwhile impact in terms of informing, persuading and building up your reputation, you will need to devise and transmit many different individual messages aimed at prospective customers, and to continue doing so for quite a long time. In fact, you will never arrive at a point where you can afford to stop contacting the customer.

GETTING THE MESSAGE ACROSS

All of us are being constantly bombarded with literally thousands of messages aimed at persuading us to buy something. To have any chance of being noticed, your particular messages must be presented in an attractive and eye-catching way. They also need to be repeated often enough to break through and be heard above the general noise and confusion of the day-to-day battle for people's attention.

Direct media advertising is one obvious way to set about this vitally-important task. Direct selling on a one-to-one basis is another possibility. The problem is that both of these methods are expensive. There are many other effective ways of influencing the customer which you should consider before looking in more detail at advertising and personal selling. These include:

- Word-of-mouth communication
- Developing a corporate identity
- Printed publicity material
- Mail shots
- Exhibitions, trade shows and demonstrations
- Special promotions
- Public relations

Word-of-mouth

One of the most important ways in which a small firm becomes more widely known is by the simple process of people talking to each other. Think about your own personal experience. What do you do if you are unfortunate enough to have a bump in the car? You might of course be a little bit accident-prone and have a long-standing relationship with a particular vehicle repair shop, but more likely you will have to start looking around to see where you can get it fixed. One of the things you are almost certain to do is to ask the people you know. In fact you probably won't have to ask — when they hear your bad luck, they will tell you without being prompted what they did when the same thing happened to them six months ago. But they do more than simply provide you with basic information on the alternatives available; what they say will influence your choice of whom you will go to for a quotation.

This kind of informal word-of-mouth communication happens all the time and applies to every type of business. The messages people pick up in this way can be positive or negative ('Don't go near so-and-so; he'll do a lousy job and you will get ripped off'). You can influence what is said about you most effectively by making sure your performance matches up with the customers expectations. But you should also pay attention to very simple things like:

- the physical appearance of your premises, your vehicles and your staff;
- the way the telephone is answered;
- the general attitude of your staff at all levels;
- your stationery, letter-headings and invoices.

Developing a corporate identity

Rightly or wrongly, people will make judgments about your business based entirely on these fairly superficial characteristics. It is highly likely that you will put off a lot of potential clients if your premises are dirty and untidy, your staff are scruffy and surly in their manner, and your office stationery is grubby and unattractive. Decent stationery is actually one of the easiest ways for a small firm to start making a good impression on people. A letter written on cheap, poor-quality paper, badly typed and with the company name printed black on white using a typeface which went out of date in the mid-1930s inevitably creates the suspicion that the service provided will also be of poor quality. There is no need to go overboard about it, but your local printer could very easily come up with some more attractive layout, using a colour and a typeface more appropriate to your particular business. Having settled on a good design, you should of course use the same colour and typeface for all your office stationery and indeed on other items like labels, stickers and packaging, and on your transport. In this way you will start the long, slow process of building up an identifiable and recognisable corporate identity.

In this context, you might also think about devising and using a company logo. This simply means an easily-remembered and visually-distinctive simple shape which people will eventually come to associate with your company and its products. It can take the form of your company name written in an unusual way (for example Ford, Esso, Coca Cola) or the initials of your company (BP, CIE), or a totally visual symbol which everyone recognises (e.g. Mercedes or Audi). The point of using a logo of some kind or other is that it provides you with a multiplicity of opportunities to draw the public's attention to your company. Think of all the different places where you come across the logo of a major multinational company—on its products, its premises, its vehicles, its stationery, its advertising and publicity material, the uniforms of its staff and so on. The same approach can make your company much better known within your own local area. However it is very important that you get it right — you may be stuck with it for a long time. If you can afford it, it is worthwhile to pay a professional design consultant or an advertising agency to advise you. One of the key points to remember is that you will want to use your logo on everything, so it should be kept simple and cheap to reproduce. There is no point whatever in having a beautiful logo which costs you a fortune every time you want to use it. The other big advantage of having a good logo is that you may be able to use it to economise on your advertising costs. By concentrating customers' recognition and recall on your company name and logo, you will avoid the trouble and expense of having to create a separate brand image for each of your products.

Figure 10. Contacting the customer

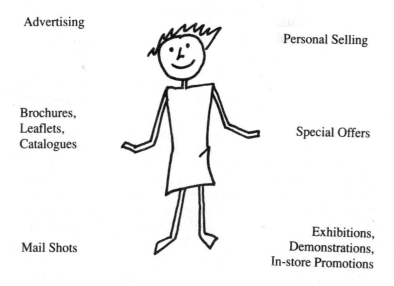

Publicity material

Well-designed and well-produced publicity material can be a very effective marketing tool for the smaller firm. Conversely, poorly-designed material can be an expensive waste of time and downright harmful to the overall image of your company. It is not too strong an assertion to say that every small firm should have some kind of leaflet, brochure or sales catalogue available. But before you dash off to the nearest printer, you should think carefully through and clarify your ideas concerning its:

- Purpose
- Readership
- Format
- Costs

It seems so obvious to ask what is the basic purpose of a leaflet or brochure, but in fact many well-intentioned efforts go badly wrong at this first hurdle, mainly through confused thinking about the job it is intended to do for you. Where does it fit in to your overall marketing activity? Consider whether your brochure is supposed to be:

- an inexpensive 'throw-away' used to answer casual enquiries, or for putting through letter-boxes in a housing estate, or for distribution at an exhibition?
- a sales-aid to be used by a representative during his or her calls, and left with the prospective customer?
- a prestige brochure aimed at establishing credibility and enhancing the corporate image?
- a document providing detailed technical information on performance and specifications?
- a mail shot?
- or what?

In defining your requirements in this area, you also need to think about who exactly the material is aimed at. Is the reader going to be a housewife, an engineer or an accountant? Remember there are a thousand other things demanding the reader's attention. Remember too that most people are not prepared to put all that much effort into reading a sales leaflet — do not presume that it will have their full and undivided attention, or that they will have the same level of interest and technical knowledge as yourself. Clarity and readability are of paramount importance, and these are strongly influenced by format and layout.

You need to decide what size and shape the item should be. It depends largely on what you want the reader to do with it. Do you want the reader to:

- read it and throw it away?
- file it for future reference?
- carry it about in a pocket or handbag?
- or what?

It is equally important to bear in mind that the non-verbal elements of a brochure (its layout, illustrations, colour, type-face, quality of paper and so on) will convey nearly as much to the reader as the actual words used. If you wish to convey the impression of a top-quality, highly-efficient outfit but attempt to do so with a badly-printed leaflet the consistency of thin toilet-paper, do not be surprised to discover that you have a credibility problem! You should also note the need for flexibility. Do not commit yourself to a format which will be out-of-date and therefore unusable in six months time — for example, prices should always be shown on a separate or detachable sheet. You should, if at all possible, employ professionals to write the copy and design the layout. This will save you a lot of time and effort. Besides, putting the two together effectively raises all sorts of technical and aesthetic problems which really are a job for specialists; trying to do it yourself is usually a false economy, unless you are very artistically talented indeed.

If you decide to include artwork or photographs, it is even more important to sub-contract the services of a specialist. Photographing a product to its best advantage is not easy, and you really need a commercial photographer — it is unlikely that your local 'weddings and parties' person will have the expertise required. You will, of course, have to give the specialists some kind of guidance, with a rough outline of what you have in mind. Bear in mind too that you do not have to accept the first proposal they come up with; do not hesitate to ask for revisions if it does not meet your needs. When you are presented with a draft, look at its overall balance, as well as checking the copy for accuracy and suitability. The visual image created by the relative positions of print, illustrations, blank spaces, heavy and light type etc. should be pleasing and stimulating. If a double-page spread is involved, the layout of the two pages should come together easily into a unified whole.

Format decisions affect budgets, and vice-versa. You really have only two options. You can say to the printer:

- This is what I want. How much is it going to cost? *or*
- This is how much I want to spend. What can you give me within that figure?

Within broad limits, the size of the print run (i.e. the total number of leaflets or brochures to be produced at one time) is not the critical factor in determining costs. More important factors are:

- the number and type of illustrations required
- the number of colours involved
- the quality of paper or board used
- preparatory design and artwork

You may resent paying out good money for something which you are after all going to give away with no guarantee of a return on your investment. Your reaction may be simply not to bother, or to opt for the cheapest (or the nearest) printer. Consider very carefully the wisdom of doing so!

Mail Shots

Having gone to the trouble and expense of acquiring some publicity material, some small firms make the mistake of not using it effectively. Mail shots can be a very efficient method of contacting the customer. As the name implies, a mail shot normally involves sending publicity material to potential customers in the post. The term 'mail shot' is however often used more loosely to include:

- inserting a leaflet in a newspaper or a magazine;
- delivering leaflets door-to-door using specialist agencies such as free local newspapers;
- leaving a supply of leaflets to be picked up by customers at sales outlets, or elsewhere.

Mail shots have a number of advantages over other methods of promoting sales such as direct media advertising. Your message can be delivered directly and personally to a specific target audience you wish to reach, as opposed to a newspaper advertisement where you have to sit back and hope that the right people will see it. Your message, for a short time at least, can command the total attention of the reader. Research has shown that the notion that most mail shots are simply dumped into the wastepaper basket unopened is simply not true. Unless it is clearly and obviously a piece of 'junk' mail which arrives regularly once a month, most people cannot resist the temptation to open a letter personally addressed to them—you never know, it just might contain a cheque!

What is true is that the mail shot must immediately command the interest of the reader; the first few lines will determine whether it is read and noted, or simply ditched. Compared with newspaper advertising, direct mail imposes fewer restrictions on the number of words, size, colour illustrations or quality of reproduction. You can, for example, include a sample of your product as part of mail shot, or some sort of discount voucher or special offer. Finally, mail shots can be relatively inexpensive in terms of their ability to guarantee contact with a specific group you have targeted. To demonstrate the point, assume for the moment that you want to inform all the farmers in a particular region about a new product or service you are about to bring onto the market. Including printing and postage costs, one letter would probably cost about fifty pence to deliver; you could be sure of reaching 1000 farmers for £500. Compare that result with what you could get for the same amount of money in other ways — a simple, relatively small advertisement in a newspaper?

However you should not expect a mail shot to produce orders directly and immediately. One of the biggest mistakes you can make is to simply bung a couple of thousand letters in the post and sit back, waiting for the business to roll in. It usually doesn't work like that; you will be lucky if you achieve more than a one or two per cent response rate. The giant mail order specialists can survive at this level through sheer volume, but it is highly unlikely that you could do so. A more sensible way to use a mail shot is to generate sales leads. Bringing your company and your product or service to the attention of a possible buyer can make life a little easier for your sales staff. In other words, the mail shot is used to open the door and is quickly followed up by telephone call or a personal visit aimed at obtaining a sales interview. With this approach, a quick follow-up is essential before the buyer forgets all about it. If you have only one or two sales people covering a large territory, and even more so if you are trying to do it on your own, it is important not to send out too many mail shots at the same time. A phased coverage is much wiser, sending out only as many letters as you can reasonably expect to follow up during the next week or so.

This, of course, does not apply to the situation where you simply want to give people a specific piece of information or raise their general level of awareness, while not requiring any response for them. In these circumstances, a mass mailing to a large number of contacts is perfectly reasonable.

The success of a mail shot depends primarily on two things:
- the impact of the letter and other material enclosed with it;
- the accuracy of the mailing list.

People tend to react fairly unfavourable to receiving an unaccompanied leaflet through the post; as a general rule it is better to include a letter. The letter should be addressed whenever possible to a named individual rather that to a company, or to, say, the 'Chief Accountant'. If you do not know the name of the Chief Accountant in a particular company, you could find out by a quick phone call. Letters which are not directed to a specific person are much more likely to be disregarded. The style in which the letter is written is also important. Keep it short, and try to grab the reader's attention in the first couple of lines. Use simple language and make sure that any introductory or special offers are explained in a way which can be easily understood. The letter should be signed personally by you, or by another senior person on your behalf — avoid the scribbled 'pp so-and-so'. Modern printing methods can make it appear that each letter has been individually signed.

Remember the need to present a good image of your company at all times — so make sure that the letter, the envelope and any other material you enclose are of the right quality.

The mailing list

It is essential to have a comprehensive and up-to-date mailing list. There is no point wasting money by sending your mail shot to people who have moved, or ceased trading, or who never existed in the first place. It is possible to rent a ready-made mailing list from various organisations, but it is better to compile your own. If you do rent (very few organisations will let you buy their mailing list outright, and this tends to be quite expensive), you may be required to use a specialist mailing firm, mainly to make sure you cannot copy the list for future use.

You may also be required to provide copies of what you are proposing to send out, just to make sure it does not include anything illegal or unpleasant.

The easiest way to start building up your own mailing list is to go through your invoices for the past year or so. Remember to avoid including any which you know are no longer relevant for one reason or another, but you should not remove someone's name simply because they have not given you an order for some time — maybe your mail shot will resurrect them for you. You can begin to add to this basic listing by including people who have requested information, or who have been identified as potential customers by your sales staff. Trade directories, lists of the membership of trade associations, even the telephone book, are other sources of useful additions.

It is naive and unrealistic to think that mail shots are a cheap and easy way to generate a large volume of business, but equally there is no doubt that, if properly used, they can be a very valuable additional marketing tool.

Exhibitions

Participation in a trade fair or exhibition because it seemed a good idea at the time is a recipe for a costly and damaging failure. You need to be

very sure that it will be worthwhile to do so before you incur the very substantial costs involved. These include:
- hiring space in the exhibition hall
- designing, constructing and removing your stand
- cleaning, insurance and hospitality
- publicity material and support advertising
- staff time, travel and subsistence

The fact of the matter is that having a stand at a big national or international exhibition is an expensive operation. Quite often, smaller firms are forced to settle for a small display in a low-cost area of the exhibition hall — and that may well prove to be counter-productive in terms of company image and customer credibility. Moreover, it is unlikely that many firm orders will result in the short term. Exhibitions tend to generate enquiries which need to be followed up at a later date. The key question you have to ask yourself is whether or not you could achieve better results by spending the same amount of money and time in other ways. Attending big exhibitions as a visitor is a useful way of doing some basic market research on competitors' activities. Doing so as an exhibitor is not usually a good idea for a smaller firm, unless you can obtain substantial grant-aid from a government agency to defray a large proportion of your costs.

However organising your own trade show is a different matter altogether. This might involve hiring a suite of rooms in a local hotel for a couple of days, setting up an attractive display, and inviting potential customers from the immediate area to come along and 'see our new product range'. Three or four such events — say in Dublin, Cork, Limerick and Belfast — would enable you to cover the whole of Ireland. You need to make sure that you do it right. Use your mailing list to send a personalised invitation to people who are good sales prospects; avoid including 'hangers-on' who are unlikely to be very much use to you. Pay careful attention to those little details that can make or break the whole thing — for example, decent lighting and appropriate hospitality. Working demonstrations are appropriate in some cases. Even where your product is too bulky or complicated for that, you can add life to the proceedings by showing a video of it in action.

In some sectors such as agricultural machinery or construction equipment, it is quite common to hire a field, erect a marquee and actually demonstrate the product in action. Another approach is to arrange for small groups of clients to visit your premises. The main advantage of all of these various kinds of DIY exhibition is that they enable you to make direct personal contact with potential customers on a one-to-one basis, thus providing a good opportunity to make a sale. A secondary advantage is that you can economise on the amount of time you devote to selling by meeting a relatively large number of clients in a few days, and by in effect having them come to you rather than the other way around.

Special Promotions

An enormously wide range of activities come under the heading of sales promotion. There is no doubt that most people are attracted by them, and they can be a useful way of increasing your sales. They tend to be used more frequently for consumer products, but are now becoming increasingly common in industrial markets as well. The great bulk of promotional activity of this kind is aimed directly at the final customer (the 'end-user'), but many sales promotions are targeted at intermediaries of one kind or another ('the trade'). Another distinction is sometimes made between promotions which have a direct and immediate impact (such as a temporary price reduction) and those which have a delayed effect (e.g. collecting trading stamps). A list of the type of sales promotions commonly used to attract consumers would include:

- Money-off special offers
- Free samples ('trial pack', perhaps attached to another product)
- Extra quantity (twenty per cent more in the pack)
- Volume discounts (buy five and get one free)
- On-pack offers (collect six labels and send away for your free coffee mug)
- Coupons and vouchers (twenty per cent off when you buy)
- Repeat purchase incentives (e.g. trading stamps or petrol station coupons)
- Competitions
- In-store demonstrations
- Special displays
- 'Free' credit

In addition to the above, sales promotions directed specifically at the trade include:

- Volume discounts ('over-riders')
- Sales contests and incentives
- Provision of display stands/cabinets
- Visits to the factory
- Sponsorship of special events (e.g. a golf competition for members of a trade association)

- Co-operative advertising
- Extended credit

In the case of trade promotions, it should be noted that it is often necessary to provide an incentive both to the distributor as a company, and also to key individuals employed by the distributor who are in a position to make things happen for you. Special promotions of this kind should not be used indiscriminately, but with a specific objective in mind such as:

- To encourage consumers to try and/or distributors to stock a new product
- To clear out old stock prior to launching a new product
- To move a slow-selling line
- To heighten the impact of an advertising campaign
- To attract a particular group of non-users or low-volume users
- To stimulate repeat purchasing
- To avoid direct competition on price
- To respond to competitive pressure
- To smooth out seasonal troughs in demand

There are however a number of disadvantages associated with this kind of activity. They can be expensive. There is always the risk that you will succeed only in provoking a fierce response from your competitors. You may only achieve a temporary increase in sales, and you may even experience a sharp drop when the promotion is withdrawn because customers have simply taken advantage of the special offer to increase their stocks and do not need to re-purchase for some time. Promotional activity can be counter-productive if used too frequently or too carelessly, with customers reacting adversely in one of two ways. Either they will think there must be something wrong with this product if it takes all this fuss to get rid of it, or alternatively they may become irritated as a result of being inundated with free plastic daffodils, or whatever. In that case, their reaction is likely to be 'Why can't they just reduce the price, rather than giving us all this rubbish we neither want nor need?' Another example of this kind of adverse reaction is the shop with the virtually permanent 'sale', which has reached a point where most people fail to notice the fact and do not believe the special offers are genuine. A final problem is that this kind of marketing activity is now so widespread that it has much less impact than was the case ten or twenty years ago. The converse of that, of course, is that if everyone else is doing it, you may be forced into a position where you cannot afford *not* to do it as well.

Some kinds of special promotions are quite frankly a waste of time and money. Many small firms give out calendars and diaries each Christmas with no real idea of why they are doing it, and well aware that most of these gifts will be passed on to somebody else, or thrown out. One wonders why they bother. Sponsorship of very small-scale and highly localised sporting or cultural events is another way of spending money without any real benefit in increased sales. However, if used properly, there is no doubt that special sales promotions are a useful additional tactical weapon in the marketing armoury.

Public Relations
PR activity is aimed primarily at bringing your company to the attention of the general public and presenting it in as favourable a light as possible. It is sometimes referred to as 'free advertising' — incorrectly, as it happens, because there are costs involved. Unless it is so small, so new or so secretive that nobody has ever heard of it, every company has a corporate image. The relevant question is whether your image is good, middling or bad. If you went out into the streets of your town and asked the first twenty people you met what they think of your company, what would they say? Perhaps the general public is not all that relevant to your particular business, and it would be more appropriate to ask a sample of key people in the trade. What kind of a reputation do you have? It is actually very important, because people are influenced by such matters when they are making purchasing decisions. They are much more likely to want to do business with a firm which has a good reputation. A good corporate image can also be helpful in your relations with government agencies, the bank, your suppliers and with your own employees.

You can influence what people think of you by developing links with local newspapers, radio and television, and by providing them with positive newsworthy stories about your firm and its activities. The opportunities are much greater than you might imagine. If you succeed in winning a big order and intend to take on a few more people — that's good news at a local level. Other examples include perhaps an award made to your company for the excellence of its product or a visit by a foreign buyer or the retirement of an employee. You may need to write up the basic facts into a press release to be sent to a few contacts. Keep it short and to the point, with a photograph where possible. It might also be useful to get to know the editor of your local paper. Many large companies regularly invite representatives of the local media to lunch just to keep them informed of what is happening. Remember that the media need stories which are after all their raw material. But remember too that adverse PR can be very destructive, and that you cannot rely on a free lunch to cover up a 'bad news' story concerning you. What do you think the Bhophal disaster in India has done for the corporate image of Union-Carbide?

DECIDING HOW MUCH TO SPEND

The money you spend on contacting the customer through advertising and other kinds of promotional activity is just as much an investment in the future of your company as buying a new machine. It is absolutely essential for your long-term survival and commercial success. Unfortunately a lot of people who run small firms cannot see it that way. The problem is partly due to the fact that you cannot guarantee a return on your marketing expenditure. When you buy a new machine, the financial sums are all very predictable. You know in advance the initial purchase price, running costs and output levels. When you set these against the anticipated reductions in costs and the revenue resulting from sales, it is fairly straightforward to make a sound judgment on whether or not it is worthwhile. You cannot do this with the marketing budget. An outlay of, say, £20,000 can be very effective or totally useless, depending on how wisely the money is spent. Then again, there is the effect on your competitor's investment in marketing. If you are spending £20,000 a year and your competitors are each spending about £2,000, you should be able to make a major impact in the market. On the other hand, if your competitors are each spending £200,000, your £20,000 will be that much less effective in generating business.

There is no easy answer to the question of how much you should spend in this area. Some managers seem to think there is some simple formula they can apply, if only they could get their hands on it. It is a fact that research has shown that the majority of firms spend between two and five per cent of turnover on advertising and sales promotion, but there are enormously wide variations in individual cases. Setting your budget as a fixed percentage of sales, or of gross profit, has the advantage of simplicity, but suffers from a major drawback when you think about it logically. This approach implies a reduction in the marketing budget when sales fall off, but common sense would suggest that this is the very moment when it should be increased. When sales go up, the marketing budget is automatically increased—but this may be unnecessary and wasteful.

The easiest approach may be described as the 'what we can afford' method. The firm's expenditure on marketing is determined by what is left in the kitty after all other commitments have been met — including perhaps repainting the toilets in the factory, and replacing the MD's car. This effectively relegates the vital task of contacting potential customers to the bottom of the list of corporate priorities. It also implies a progressive reduction in marketing activity as the firm slides deeper into trouble through falling sales, which again is not the most sensible thing to do.

Another alternative is to take a guess at roughly how much your competitors are spending and set your budget more or less on a par with them. This only makes sense if your firm and theirs are exactly the same in every respect, which is highly unlikely. Even then it is a recipe for maintaining the status quo by adopting an essentially negative and defensive posture. Besides, if your main competitors are much bigger than you are, you will not be able to keep up with them. In this situation, you need to be more imaginative in allocating your more limited resources to maximum effect.

The most sensible way to go about this is usually referred to as the 'objective and task' approach. This involves four steps.

- Define your marketing objectives as precisely as you can.
- Think carefully about what specific activities you need to undertake in order to achieve these objectives.
- Cost out what is needed to implement them.
- Decide whether, given your limited resources, it is realistic to set your budget at that level.

If the answer is 'no', go back to the start and set more limited objectives. Repeat the process until you are able to give a 'yes' answer at the end.

This procedure is not easy, and you should not allow yourself to become bogged down in a tangled mess of fine details. You may not have access to the detailed information on costs you would need to do it really accurately. You may find it difficult to express your objectives clearly. But setting about it in this way, even with a very broad brush, is far better than simply pulling figures out of the air. If nothing else, it will force you to think about what you are trying to achieve through your marketing efforts and how you are going to go about it.

Summary of Key Points
1. You need to make sure that every potential customer is aware of your existence and of what you have to offer.
2. You need to define as precisely as you can what sort of people you need to contact (your 'target audience') and the best way of reaching them.

3. You need to decide what message you want to convey. It should include basic information about who you are, what you offer and where you can be found. It may also involve an element of persuasion — giving people sound reasons why they should buy from you rather than from one of your competitors.
4. There are many different ways of conveying your message to potential customers, including advertising, personal selling, printed publicity material, mail shots, exhibitions, trade shows, demonstrations and special promotions of one kind or another.
5. It is useful to develop a corporate image which people will immediately recognise. This takes a long time and may involve designing a company logo and house style which is used on *everything*—packaging, letter-headings, advertisements, vehicles and so on.
6. Well-designed and well-produced leaflets, brochures and sales catalogues can be very effective and relatively inexpensive marketing aids for the smaller firms. Conversely, poorly-designed, cheap-looking material can be downright harmful to your image.
7. Mail shots are a useful and inexpensive way of making yourself more widely known and generating enquiries. But they are not a substitute for selling, and are not a very effective way of obtaining firm orders. It is a mistake to send out a couple of thousand leaflets in the post, and then sit back waiting for the orders to roll in — they usually don't.
8. Having a stand at a major trade fair or exhibition is expensive, and not usually a good idea for the small firm unless substantial assistance from a government agency is available. Organising your own mini-exhibition in a local hotel is much more cost-effective.
9. The term 'sales promotion' covers a very wide range of activities, including special cut-price offers, free samples, volume discounts, free gifts, competitions, displays and demonstrations. Done well, these are a very effective way of attracting the customer's attention, but they should only be used to achieve a specific objective. Too frequent sales promotions can be counter-productive.
10. Money invested in contacting the customer is just as important as buying a new machine; but you must take care to spend your money wisely. Think carefully through and decide what objectives you are trying to achieve, and what is the most cost-effective way of going about it.

A Case History
A talented young electrical engineer set up his own business manufacturing components which were incorporated into the much larger pieces of equipment made by the Irish subsidiary of a major multinational. Initially things went very well, and after ten years he had built up a reasonably prosperous company employing thirty-five people. Then disaster struck. His major customer, which accounted for ninety-five per cent of his sales, was taken over. The new owners decided that all components would henceforth be shipped in from their main plant in the United States. As part of a programme to slim down the workforce, they also made redundant the Purchasing Manager who had been instrumental in channelling a lot of business to small local sub-contractors.

It is scarcely surprising to note that the young engineer was devastated. At one stroke, the whole basis of his business had been destroyed. Fortunately he had built up a small surplus to re-equip, which he could draw upon to provide some kind of breathing space, and he still had a few outstanding orders to complete. The bottom line was quite simple — he needed some new customers, and quickly. Otherwise he was finished.

In fact, he was very ill-equipped to search for new business. He had never done any market research in his life; nor had he ever really had to do any selling — his cosy chats with his old friend the Purchasing Manager scarcely count. He did not have a sales catalogue or even a price-list.

When his initial panic had subsided, he worked through the phone book to draw up a list of possible customers, which he defined as firms making the same kind of equipment as his former customer. The initial trawl produced a very short list indeed — in fact there were only two names on it — so he tried again. This time he listed any firm, government department or semi-state agency which might conceivably have a need for the kind of components he could produce, or might be using machinery including these components which he could service or refurbish. This much broader view of the nature of his business produced a substantially longer list of possible clients.

The next problem was how to contact them. He tackled it by printing a brochure which basically said: 'Here I am, and this is what I can do'. He posted this to all the clients on his list and waited for the phone to ring. Nothing happened. So he tried again. This time he took the trouble to find out the name of the Managing Director, the Production Manager or the Chief Engineer of the organisations on his list, and wrote to each of them personally. He followed this up with a phone call asking for a meeting. He drew a blank with about eighty per cent of them — but he ended up with about a dozen people who were prepared to see him. The problem then was how to make a decent sales pitch to each of these potential customers. He approached this by finding out in advance as much as he could about the nature of their business, and then thinking hard about what he might conceivably offer.

This true story has a happy ending, in that he did eventually manage to broaden substantially both his customer base and his product range. The business is once again profitable, and its prospects are much healthier now that all its eggs are not in a single basket.

8.
Advertising

The main advantage of direct media advertising is that it enables you to contact a large number of potential customers at one time. A particular advertisement will be seen or read by literally thousands of people, in some cases millions. Its main disadvantage is that it can be quite costly. As a rough general rule, the more people who are likely to see an advertisement, the more expensive it will be to run it. A full-scale nationwide advertising campaign to launch a new consumer product can cost several million pounds. The average small firm is obviously not in that league. It simply could not afford that kind of money. The chances also are that it could not cope with the volume of sales likely to result from advertising at that level.

In fact, a small firm may not need to advertise at all — but that statement requires some hasty clarification. It is absolutely essential that you contact a sufficient number of potential buyers to generate the orders you need to stay in business and make a profit. However there are many ways of contacting the customer other than through direct media advertising. Some of these alternatives were discussed in the previous chapter, and the next chapter is concerned with another very important method of doing so — personal selling. The basic point to bear in mind is that advertising is only one of a number of methods of communicating with potential customers available in the marketing tool-kit. You can decide to use it or not, depending on your own particular circumstances. If you decide that advertising is appropriate to your needs, there are a number of things you will have to think about before you rush out to spend some of your hard-earned cash.

- What is the purpose of your advertising?
- Where should you advertise?
- What sort of advertising do you need?
- How often should you advertise?
- How can you find out if your advertising is effective?
- Do you need to use an advertising agency?

THE PURPOSE OF ADVERTISING

The basic purpose underlying any kind of advertising is to generate sales. But that broad general statement covers a wide range of specific objectives. These include:

- letting people know who you are, what you have to offer and where you are to be found;
- convincing them of the merits of a particular product or service;
- telling them about a new product or service, and persuading them to try it;
- providing specific information about a special offer;
- holding on to existing customers in the face of intense competitive activity;
- changing the image people have of your company.

You need to be absolutely clear in your own mind about what exactly you are trying to achieve when you run a series of advertisements. Taking as an example the last of the possible objectives listed above, the owner of a garden centre discovered recently that most people in his catchment area believed that his prices were much higher than those of his competitors. He was able to satisfy himself that this was simply not true across most of his product range. When he had calmed down a bit (his first reaction was outraged indignation at the injustice of it), he ran a series of advertisements on the theme of 'good value for money', including several very attractive special offers. Business picked up substantially as a result. The purpose of advertising is to inform and persuade. But in planning your advertising, you need to refine this into a much more precise statement of your objectives. This will involve defining as accurately as you can:

- the target audience you want to reach;
- the message you want to convey to them.

WHERE SHOULD YOU ADVERTISE?

The simplest answer is that you should advertise in whatever medium provides the best opportunity of reaching your target audience at a cost you can afford. The range of advertising media currently available in Ireland is as wide as anywhere else in the world. It includes:

- Television and radio
- National, regional and local newspapers
- 'Free' newspapers
- Magazines, both general interest and specialist
- Trade journals

- Directories, handbooks and other reference material (e.g. telephone book)
- Posters and billboards
- Transport
- Cinema
- Odds and ends (e.g. carrier bags, boxes of matches and so on)
- Sponsorship

You have two quite separate decisions to make at an early stage in planning your advertising. You must choose:

- between media (e.g. TV or radio or newspaper)
- within media (e.g. Which newspaper)

The factors you should take into consideration when making these choices are:

- Coverage
- Costs
- Compatibility
- Competitive activity

Coverage

If you look at what large firms do, you will see that most consumer products and services are heavily advertised on television, in the national press and in the higher circulation weekly magazines. The usual advice given to small firms is that using the mass media is far too expensive and totally unthinkable for most of them. This is not necessarily true in a small country like Ireland. It is usually out of the question for a small firm to think in terms of a series of thirty second television commercials, or full-page spreads in the Sunday newspapers. Quite apart from the hefty bill for running advertisements of this kind, there are major costs associated with preparing them. But it is not unrealistic within the context of a relatively low advertising budget to use television on a more limited scale — for example, with the sort of commercials which are in effect a single colour slide with a brief message read by the announcer, perhaps with appropriate music in the background. Again, quite large advertisements in regional or local newspapers are not nearly as expensive as you might think.

As a general rule, products and services which are sold to other companies as opposed to the general public are not nearly as heavily advertised as consumer products. The promotional effort tends to be concentrated on the activities of sales representatives, supplemented with appropriate publicity material and participation in trade shows and exhibitions. Direct advertising is often limited to the trade press, i.e. highly specialist publications geared to the needs of a particular industrial sector.

The key point to remember is that you must choose the media which will best convey your message to the target audience you wish to contact. You need to ensure that you are reaching the maximum possible number of the right sort of people. You can waste a lot of money by making the wrong choice. If you are selling, let us say, fishing tackle, you could no doubt contact a lot of fishermen by an advertisement in a daily newspaper. But the great majority of people who see it will never be converted into customers, no matter how appealing the message is. A much more cost-effective approach would be to advertise in one (or all) of the specialist magazines for fishing enthusiasts. You need to apply the same kind of thinking to your business.

- Whom exactly do I want to contact?
- What kind of newspaper or magazine are they likely to read?
- What television and radio programmes would they be interested in?
- Given the amount of money I have available, where is the best place for me to advertise?

Information on the size and nature of the audience reached by the various media is readily available. There are a number of directories which give circulation or viewing figures, advertising rates and data on the audience characteristics of every television company, radio station, newspaper and magazine in the British Isles, but you may well have trouble in getting hold of them. Copies are sometimes kept in the reference section of main public libraries, but it is much easier to simply pick up the phone and ask whichever newspaper or magazine you are interested in to send you their rate-card. You will find that they are more than happy to provide this kind of information — selling advertising space is after all one of their major sources of revenue. Just bear in mind that they will of course present themselves in the best possible light, and you may require a pinch of salt when you look at what they claim. You can rely on 'audited' figures giving the coverage of the main newspapers, magazines, television and radio, because these are independently verified; unaudited circulation figures of some of the smaller specialist magazines and trade journals can be a little suspect. Another point to bear in mind is the distinction between circulation (the total number of copies sold) and readership (the estimated total number of people who see a particular edition). But remember that not all readers (or viewers or listeners) are necessarily potential customers. Some element of wastage is inevitable.

Costs

There is a straight trade-off between the number of people you can reach through a particular advertising medium and the costs involved in doing so — the bigger the audience, the higher the costs. To put this into some kind of perspective, showing a thirty second commercial on RTE 1 at peak viewing time could cost as much as £3000 if you want to guarantee a specific slot (say, just before or just after the main evening news). But it will be seen by about 1,750,000 people. The same commercial could cost about £2500 on UTV and £2000 on RTE 2, reflecting the rather smaller audience reached. However, all the television companies give substantial discounts for a series of advertisements, offering special rates for first-time advertisers. For example, a ten second spot on RTE 1 can cost as little as £250 in the evening, and around £100 in the afternoon. These figures show that television advertising is not beyond the reach of the average small firm, although clearly it is simply not on to think of a major campaign involving the production of perhaps three or four full-length commercials and showing them at peak viewing time over several weeks — that could easily cost half a million pounds.

Turning to the newspapers, a full page advertisement costs about £11,000 in the *Irish Times* or the *Irish Independent*, £7500 in the Dublin *Evening Press*, and about £5000 in the *Cork Examiner* or the *Belfast Telegraph*. In contrast, a full page in a local weekly paper would cost about £1000, and in some cases as little as £500. Smaller advertisements obviously cost much less, on a more or less pro-rata basis.

A rough and ready way of assessing the relative merits of different advertising media is to work out the 'cost per 1000' — in other words the advertising cost per 1000 people reached by a given advertisement. This is useful in helping you to decide which one to go for, but it has some obvious disadvantages. It is unwise to assume that every reader or viewer will actually see your particular advertisement. An unknown proportion (but less than 100 per cent) of them will notice it, and a still smaller proportion will be able to recall the contents accurately twenty-four hours later. Cost per 1000 also does not take into account the qualitative aspects of advertising — a well-designed, imaginative advertisement will have a much greater impact than a poor one, even though the costs of running them are exactly the same.

Big companies can afford to employ someone in their marketing department to specialise in the complicated art of media buying, or pay an advertising agency to do it for them. That luxury is not available for the small firm. Unfortunately for them (because it involves more time and effort), the only answer is to get hold of and carefully assess the information provided by the various media on costs and coverage to make sure that the best possible deal is obtained.

Compatibility

Different media have different characteristics and appeal to different groups of people. It is important to make sure that your message is communicated through channels which fit in with the characteristics of your product or service, and with the image of the company you want to promote. To give a very simple example, it is hardly appropriate to advertise heavy-duty arc welding gear in a women's weekly magazine. That course of action is so obviously wrong from just about every angle — target audience, general atmosphere, costs — that it is hard to imagine anybody actually doing it. It is worth taking a few moments to have a look at the characteristics, advantages and disadvantages of the main media.

Television

The power of television as a method of advertising is due to the fact that colour, movement and sound can be employed in a way which is not possible elsewhere. It is a basic fact of the way human beings are built that we notice something in full colour much more quickly than if it is presented only in black and white, and we notice something which is moving much more quickly than if it is static. Therein lies the power of television advertising. Many products benefit from television's ability to demonstrate them in use (e.g. a vacuum cleaner or a car). But many television advertisements are aimed at creating a positive brand image and ensuring instantaneous recognition of the product on the shelves of the supermarket. Ask yourself who actually sells most customer products to the housewife. It is not the check-out girl, nor indeed is it anybody else in the retail outlet. It is hard to imagine someone approaching a woman in a supermarket to say 'Excuse me madam, could I interest you in a tin of soup?' The main selling job is done by advertising, primarily on television, although of course attractive packaging and efficient merchandising have a part to play.

The other major advantage of television is the sheer size of the audience that can be reached. However, the medium also suffers from several disadvantages. The high costs of producing advertisements are often overlooked, as is the need for multiple repetition. A television commercial is displayed for only a few seconds; it needs to be shown frequently to make sure that the maximum number of people see it. The audience tends to include a large number of people who are not part of the target audience you wish to contact, although it is possible to be selective by a careful choice of timing.

Radio
Commercial radio can provide easy access to a highly localised audience. With careful planning, a high degree of selectivity can be achieved. A primarily male business and professional audience can be reached by advertising concentrated into the morning and evening 'drive to work' times; housewives tend to listen mid-morning or mid-afternoon and so on. The main disadvantages are the same as for television — the message is very short, and multiple repetitions are required if it is to have any worthwhile impact. A further disadvantage is that the product is not visually displayed.

Newspapers and magazines
National newspapers offer the considerable advantage of being able to reach huge numbers of people. It is possible to target broad customer groups in terms of their social class and other characteristics (as by placing advertisements aimed at women on the women's features page, or for sporting goods on the sports pages). However, these are quite expensive and have a very short life-span — nobody reads yesterday's newspaper. Local weekly newspapers tend to be around the house for much longer, advertising costs are much lower, and they provide access to a particular geographical area. The primary purpose of highly localised free newspapers is to carry advertising rather than hard news. This can be a very cost-effective medium indeed for the small firm.

Consumer magazines tend to be of two kinds. First, there are the high circulation weeklies aimed at a broad segment of the market — the best examples perhaps are those designed to appeal to women. Their advantages include the ability to target fairly precisely, the availability of high quality colour printing and their relatively long life. Disadvantages are that their advertising rates can be expensive and they tend to be dominated by the advertisements of large companies. Secondly, there are the much lower circulation specialist magazines of which there are literally hundreds. If you want to target just about any specific sub-group of consumers — golfers, pop-music fans, young mothers — you can usually find an appropriate publication to enable you to do so. Specialist trade journals offer a relatively cheap way of contacting a readership

128 Marketing for the Small Business in Ireland

Figure 11. Newspaper advertising

Classified

Display

Semi-display

which you can be certain are interested in products and services relevant to that particular sector. For that reason these are a very good bet for the small firm. The only disadvantage is that most of your competitors, both large and small, will also be using them.

Directories
The big advantage of directories of one kind or another is that they are consulted by people who are actively looking for potential suppliers of whatever product or service they are interested in. Advertising rates are relatively inexpensive, the message stays alive for a long time, and a steady flow of new, potential customers will see it. A disadvantage is that long lists of names and addresses are not exactly eye-catching, and it is probably worthwhile to pay the extra cost required to make your entry stand out a bit from the crowd.

Outdoor Advertising
Outdoor advertising in the form of posters on hoardings, buses and so on must be bold and brief — the average car driver or passenger will have only a few seconds to notice it. Only a limited amount of information can be presented and it must be displayed with absolute clarity on an appropriate site and be big enough to be seen from a distance. All very obvious — but take a look around you when you are driving to work some morning. You may be surprised at how many amateur advertisers are wasting their time by failing to observe these simple rules. The other advantage of outdoor advertising is the likelihood that the message will be seen frequently and for quite a long time.

Cinemas
Cinema advertising can be quite useful for some products and services, particularly those aimed at young people. Provided you avoid the cinema equivalent of the full-scale television commercial, costs are fairly low and you have a captive audience with few distractions.

Sponsorship
Sponsorship of sporting or cultural events is something which needs to be done on a large scale to have any real effect, and is therefore not a viable alternative for a smaller firm. Presenting a new set of jerseys to your village football team might make you feel good. It might even get your picture into the local paper — but it is unlikely to increase your sales very much. Similarly, small-scale advertising by means of books of matches, ball pens and so on is not particularly cost-effective.

Competitive Activity

Everyone tends to think of advertising as a way of increasing sales, but from time to time its strategic purpose may be to avoid a reduction in your sales. It may be unwise to allow your competition to have uncontested access to a particular group of potential customers, or to fail to respond when they increase the level of their advertising. The nature of your response will be determined mainly by the amount of spare cash you have available. This is one of the reasons why it is always useful to build a contingency allowance into your overall budget. However, it is a major mistake to adopt a purely defensive posture, reacting only to what others do. You should make up your mind what you want to do — and go for it!

WHAT SORT OF ADVERTISING?

Advertising is essentially a creative process involving the imaginative use of verbal and non-verbal elements (colour, sound, movement, the effect of different type faces, and so on). There is an almost infinite range of different possible combinations of these various elements. The problem is how to sort out which particular combination is likely to be successful in achieving your objectives, given the constraints on the amount of time and money you have available. It is useful to think about it at two different levels:

- the broad approach you are going to adopt
- the detailed mechanics of doing so

Alternative approaches to advertising

There are three broad approaches you need to think about before you decide what sort of advertising is best for you:

- the purely informative approach
- the Unique Selling Proposition (USP) approach
- the brand image approach

You may decide that your purposes are best served by simple direct advertisements which provide basic information to potential customers. In many situations, all that is required is to let them know what you have to offer and where you may be found. But most advertising tries to go a bit further than that by adding to the basic information an attempt to persuade the customer to choose a particular version of the product or service in question.

The USP approach

A very common and time-honoured way of doing so is by emphasising those benefits and features of your product or service which you believe people will find attractive. In other words, you give them a number of solid reasons why they should buy from you, rather than simply telling them what they can buy. This is sometimes referred to as the Unique Selling Proposition method of advertising. In its purest form, the USP approach requires the following.

- Each advertisement should make a specific proposition to the customer — buy this and you will derive this benefit.
- The proposition must, if at all possible, be unique, i.e. not also offered by competitors.
- The proposition must be sufficiently attractive to motivate people to buy the product.
- The proposition must be credible — otherwise it will be ignored.

Many radically different propositions can be devised for any product or service. These range from straightforward claims that this is the least expensive version on the market, or is the best value for money, or has the lowest running costs, right through to more complicated propositions based on emotional or social appeals (e.g. 'all the best people use—'). It is of course totally impossible to tell you here and now what USPs would be suitable for you to use in your advertising. What you need to do is to think imaginatively about the sort of benefits you can offer and to emphasise them in your advertisements. The more you can dream up, the better will be your chances of making a real impact — but do not try and pile all possible USPs into every single advertisement. It is usually better to spread them out a bit, concentrating on only two or three things at any one time. Remember too that you can be prosecuted or otherwise taken to task for making claims that are grossly misleading or simply untrue.

The Brand Image Approach

The third option is to create a brand image for your product or service. Brand image could be defined as all those emotional and aesthetic qualities that people have come to associate with a particular brand. It is probably easier to get the hang of it by thinking about a well-known brand. What sort of product attributes spring to mind when you think about, say, Hamlet cigars, or a Bounty bar, or a Volvo? Brand image advertising does not usually provide any hard information about the product at all. Instead, it concentrates on creating favourable associations in the mind of the consumer and in making the product immediately recognisable. Hamlet and Bounty advertisements do not tell you what the product is made of, how much it costs, or where you can buy it — but they are very, very effective in stimulating sales. Creating a brand image takes a long time and costs a lot of money. For this reason, it is an approach which small firms should adopt only after very careful consideration of what is involved. However, it is perfectly possible for a small firm to build a sound brand image for its product in a limited geographical area, through attractive packaging, effective merchandising and some media advertising.

The Mechanics of Advertising

Small firms have to think in terms of advertisements which achieve the best possible impact for the least possible outlay. In the case of television, that usually means using ten-second 'slide with voice-over' spots rather than full-scale commercials. The television companies will use their production facilities to create your advertisements for you, using your ideas (if you have any) and your specification of the basic message you want to get across. There are also many small independent production companies which will do the same job — you can find them in the phone book. The costs are not particularly high — about £350 per advertisement at current rates.

In newspapers, the basic unit by which advertising space is sold is the single column centimetre (scc). The most basic way in which space can be bought is in the 'classified section' — the one-column-wide lists of used cars and so on which you will see in any paper you care to pick up. If that is all you can afford, you can console yourself that a surprisingly high proportion of readers do actually look at classified ads, and they can be quite an effective way of generating sales. However, if at all possible, you should think in terms of 'display' advertising. This means blocks of varying sizes — for example 15 cm x 2 columns, or 20 cm x 3 columns — which provide an opportunity to make use of larger print and illustrations of one kind or another. Here again, most newspapers will design an attractive layout for you — at a fee, of course. Within the general rule that advertising rates for different papers vary in proportion to their circulation, the costs of advertising in a given newspaper will be affected by:

- the size of the advertisement
- its position in the paper
- the number of times it appears

You will not be surprised to discover that a bigger advertisement will cost you more, but you may not be aware that advertisements of a given size have different prices according to the page on which they appear and the position on that page. The reason for this is the belief that people pay more attention to some pages and are therefore more likely to see an advertisement there rather than elsewhere in the paper. It is difficult to give specific advice on which pages are best from this point of view, because the format and lay-out of newspapers varies so widely. A useful guide is provided by the relative costs shown in their rate-card, which any newspaper will be happy to send you. However, the fact of the matter is that a lot of the advice you may encounter on which space in a newspaper is most effective is based on suppositions and heresay rather than on hard scientific evidence. There is a school of thought which argues that if an advertisement is big enough and attractive enough, it will be noticed wherever it appears.

For what it's worth, the conventional wisdom about the optimal size and placing of an advertisement in a technical or trade magazine is that it should:

- appear in the first third of the publication
- on the right-hand page
- on a page containing news or other editorial matter
- be at least one-third of a page in size

The costs of such an advertisement should be well within the budget of any small firm. But a more important key to success is choosing the right journal — the one which is read by most of the influential people in their particular line of business.

HOW OFTEN SHOULD YOU ADVERTISE?

The single answer is: as often as you need to to make sure your message is getting through. What you must bear in mind is that a single isolated advertisement on its own is likely to achieve very little. Quite frankly, if that's all you can afford, you would probably be better to spend your money on some other method of generating sales. Your advertisements have to compete with thousands of others in attracting the attention of your target audience — that is why it is so vitally important to have good copy and artwork. But another aspect of advertising's overall impact is the frequency with which people see your message. In a very real sense, advertising is a learning process. The greater the number of repetitions, the greater are the chances of the message getting through and being retained. First of all, you need to break through the general noise and confusion and grab the attention of potential customers. Then you must keep hammering home your message to make sure they do not forget it.

Big companies selling consumer products advertise heavily and continuously in the mass media. They rely on the cumulative effect of multiple repetition to make sure their customers are thoroughly familiar with their brands. There is no way a small firm could afford to become involved in this ongoing battle for market share. Small firms need to be a lot more astute than this in allocating their more limited advertising budget. A viable strategy for them to follow is to go in hard and make as big an impact as possible for a short period of time, and then follow this up with regular reminder advertising on a more limited scale until the next time they can afford to make a fairly big splash. The reasoning behind this 'intermittent bursts' approach goes right back to the idea of advertising as a learning process for the customer. Provided your advertising has sufficient impact to be noticed in the first place, the initial learning of your message takes place fairly quickly, but forgetting occurs at a rather slower rate — hence the need for regular reminders.

In contrast, small firms which sell primarily to other companies are more likely to advertise in less expensive media such as trade journals. They may well be able to afford to do so on a regular and continuous basis. Just remember that if you fall into this category, you will need to change the layout and content of your advertisements from time to time. If you persist in using the same advertisement, people will become so used to seeing it that they will no longer take any notice of it. In a way, it becomes part of the furniture — they are vaguely aware that it is there, but simply ignore it.

Another aspect of the timing of your advertising is that there may be seasonal fluctuations in your trade which you have to take into account. This may well involve, for example, advertisements focussed on certain products at the start of the summer and on different ones in late autumn to account for winter purchasing. There is always, of course, the pre-Christmas season scrum, but you should think carefully before you dive into it. There is a very real risk that your relatively puny efforts will simply be overwhelmed in the general pandemonium. You might have a better chance of being noticed if you hold off your main effort until a quieter time of the year — but not in the middle of August when most people are away on holiday.

Assessing the effectiveness of advertising
You may well be thinking that there is little or no point in trying to measure how effective your advertising has been. After all, the money

has been spent and there is nothing you can do about it. There *is* something you can do about it — do better next time round.

It also makes a lot of sense to test your advertising before it goes out. This can be done quite simply be showing your mock-ups and proofs to a few people and inviting them to comment on whether or not they understand it, like its visual impact and so on. Make sure the people you ask are similar to your target audience — your fifty-year-old accountant is not the best person to judge if an advertisement is likely to be attractive to teenage girls. Do not be afraid to change things if you find you are getting negative feedback. Even though late changes will probably involve additional costs, this will be less expensive in the long run than going ahead with an ineffective advertisement

Once your campaign is under way, there are two quite separate aspects that you might find it worthwhile to look at:
- communication effectiveness
- sales effectiveness

You need to know if your advertising has been successful in conveying the message you want to get across. There are various techniques available to do this. Big firms spend a lot a money commissioning market research agencies to undertake detailed studies of the communications effectiveness of their advertising. That is not a viable option for most small firms and you may well have to rely on a less scientific approach. Here again the best approach is to simply ask around. You should try to establish what level of recognition and recall you have succeeded in creating. In other words, can people drawn from your target audience remember having seen your advertisements? If so, can they recall with any degree of accuracy what was in them? If the answer is 'no' to either or both of these questions, you have a problem.

Even if most people can remember seeing your advertising, you may still have a problem. It can happen that a series of advertisements is very successful in communicating a particular message, but this achievement is not subsequently matched by any significant increase in sales volume. Some advertising of course is not aimed at generating an immediate rise in sales. But if that is your objective, it is worth keeping an eye on what is happening. If your sales have increased substantially in the weeks and months following your advertising campaign, it is not unreasonable to infer that your advertising has been effective. Unfortunately it is not quite as simple as that. Your sales may have gone up in spite of your advertising rather than because of it. Your advertising may have succeeded in preventing your sales from going down in the face of intense competition from your rivals.

The fact of the matter is that it is extremely difficult to measure the effectiveness of advertising with any real degree of accuracy, even by using the most sophisticated research techniques currently available. Someone is supposed to have said, 'I know that half the money I spend on advertising is wasted — the trouble is, I don't know which half'. This person's assessment was absolutely right.

USING AN ADVERTISING AGENCY
Your decision on whether you need to employ the services of an advertising agency depends largely on the size of your marketing budget, and how much of it is spent on advertising as opposed to other ways of contacting the customer. If your annual advertising spending is quite high, say £50,000 a year or more, you will find it very useful to channel it through an agency and let them deal with the various tasks involved on your behalf. On the other hand, if you spend very little on direct media advertising, it is probably not worth your while to use an agency. In fact you may well have some difficulty in finding one that is prepared to take you on — advertising agencies tend to take the view that very small accounts are far more trouble than they are worth. But you should not jump to the conclusion that you do not need specialist help. To avoid the major mistake of making do with amateurish and ineffective DIY advertisements, you will need to sub-contract graphic designers, printers, professional copy-writers and so on. Three questions need to be answered before you reach a final decision.
- What can an advertising agency do for you?
- How are they paid?
- How should you select an agency?

The Role of an Advertising Agency
The main function of an advertising agency is to bring together all the specialist skills needed by their clients. A good agency can:
- advise on a company's overall marketing strategy
- plan advertising campaigns
- book space in the media
- produce advertisements and other publicity material
- carry out market research

One of the major advantages in using an agency is that fresh minds with a lot of experience in different sectors are brought to bear on your particular marketing problems. That does not mean that you can simply dump on them the decisions about where you want your company to go and how you propose to get there. Responsibility for your long-term strategy must remain firmly with you. But there is some truth in the old saying about not being able to see the wood for the trees. Managers who are up to their ears in the day-to-day problems of running a business sometimes find it difficult to stand back and look afresh at the direction in which they are headed. It is often helpful to have a second opinion from an informed, objective and sympathetic observer. A lot of expertise is also needed to work out the detail of an advertising campaign and to ensure that all the various elements of it come together according to plan. One particular aspect of this is media scheduling — the complex task of allocating the available budget between different media, obtaining the best deal, booking the appropriate space or air time to make sure of contacting the target audience, and paying the bills.

Above all else, an agency must be creative. It must have on its staff people with the ability to use words, sounds and pictures imaginatively to project an idea in such a way that it has real impact in the market place. A number of different skills are required to achieve the overall effect. Copywriters are responsible for the words used. They are the people who dream up the unforgettable slogans which become imprinted on people's minds. They also have the more mundane task of describing the details of technical performance concisely and clearly. The art director (sometimes called the visualiser) and graphic designers are responsible for the visual aspects of the proposed advertisement. The copywriters and the visualiser must work together as a team. They must consider a host of facts and impressions about the product or service being advertised, the market segment it is aimed at, the media which will be used and the competition it will face.

The end result of their efforts should be an original and relevant way of expressing the desired message and/or projecting the desired company or brand image so that it will reach the people at whom it is directed, while standing out from the other distractions competing for their attention. This will be presented to the client for approval in the form of mock-ups which bring together the proposed artwork and copy. In the case of television, the end result will be a detailed script and an illustrated story board showing the sequence of visual images which will be followed. If clients are not entirely happy with the result, they should raise their doubts at this point — doing so later on is much more expensive.

Once the creative team has obtained the go-ahead from the client, other specialists take over the task of actually producing the advertisement in a form compatible with the printing process to be used, or as a film suitable for television or cinema advertising. Printed publicity material also needs to be designed and produced.

Quite often these jobs are sub-contracted to smaller highly-specialised firms, and the role of the agency is primarily to make sure they do a good job. For example, agency print production supervisors are responsible for the quality of all material printed for the agency and its clients. Their task is to see that the copy comes up crisp and clear, that the artwork which looked so effective in the design studio is accurately reproduced, and that the colouring and detail of photographs painstakingly shot by skilled commercial photographers do not lose their quality when they appear in print. Many agencies also offer to carry out market research on behalf of their clients, but this too is usually sub-contracted to a specialist agency.

Advertising agencies organise themselves in many different ways to cope with their complex range of tasks. Most of them operate a system in which one of their employees acts as the link between the agency and the client. This person is usually referred to as the account executive, or the client executive, and is quite often a young graduate with two or three years' experience in the advertising business. It is a difficult job to do well, in that the account executives have to reconcile the sometimes conflicting needs and wishes of both their clients and their colleagues within the agency. It is essential that account executives are fully briefed on all aspects of the client's activities, and is kept informed of changes in thinking and policy. They must also command the respect of their specialist colleagues and make sure that they work together effectively as a team to achieve the clients' objectives.

Regular meetings between the client executive and the client are needed to ensure that both parties fully understand and agree what these objectives actually are. The busy manager should not make the mistake of simply leaving the agency to get on with it after a couple of quick chats about what may be required — the likely outcome of that kind of 'hands off' approach is that the agency will not produce the desired result. At the same time, the client must avoid the temptation to interfere too much in the detail of the creative and design work for which the agency was employed in the first place. But ultimately, the person who pays the bills has the final say in deciding what is acceptable.

Paying an Advertising Agency

Agencies earn a commission from the advertising media in respect of their total billings (i.e. the total amount of space or air-time purchased in a given period). The straight commission system works quite well in the case of big companies marketing fast-moving consumer goods and with substantial advertising budgets to spend. Most small companies do not spend enough on direct media advertising to make this a viable method of recovering the costs involved in servicing their account. It also suffers the major disadvantage from the point of view of a small firm that there is a in-built temptation for an agency to recommend the maximum possible amount of direct media advertising as opposed to other kinds of promotional activity which do not yield commission.

For these reasons, payment of an annual retainer for basic services plus additional fees for specific tasks undertaken on behalf of the client is the most common contractual relationship between a small company and an advertising agency in Ireland, both North and South, at the present time. This sort of arrangement encourages the agency to give truly impartial advice, but it is essential to agree right at the outset exactly what services will be provided for the basic fee and what will be regarded as extras. There is likely to be a wide variation in the scale of fees quoted by different agencies for what appears to be more or less the same service. Before coming to a firm arrangement, the agency should be asked to prepare a written statement setting out clearly what has been agreed, along with its basis for calculating the fee to be charged. Most will be happy to do so, if only to avoid the risk of protracted wrangling when their invoices are presented to the client for payment.

Choosing an Advertising Agency

Many small firms set about the job of finding and appointing an advertising agent in a fairly haphazard way. Quite often what happens is that they approach an agency which has been recommended by a friend or business associate, and enter into an ill-defined relationship after a single brief meeting. That is not the most sensible way to go about it. The task of appointing someone to handle your advertising should be approached in the same way as the appointment of any other employee. You would not for one moment consider offering the job of Production Manager to someone you hardly know without considering other applicants and without taking up references from previous employers. You would also have, or should have, a job description setting out what you want the person appointed to do for you.

You should follow the same approach in appointing an advertising agency. Before you start the selection process, you need to sort out in your own mind what you are looking for. It is well worthwhile to try writing down a list of the specific tasks you want the agency to handle on your behalf. After all, if you are not terribly sure about what you want, it is a little unfair to throw your hands up in disgust if eventually you get something different from what you finally decide is really needed. You should then draw up a short-list of agencies to approach, based on firm evidence of their experience and creative abilities. There is much to be said for employing a smaller, locally-based agency rather than a nationally or internationally-known big name, if only on the grounds that you are more likely to be given the attention you deserve if you are an important part of the agency's total client portfolio. This particular problem is perhaps less likely to arise in a small country like Ireland than elsewhere. Finding out the names of possible contacts is easy — you need only look in the phone book — but a word of warning is needed at this point.

There is absolutely nothing in law to prevent anyone at all from setting themselves up in business as a 'marketing consultant'. There are unfortunately some charlatans around whose abilities and qualifications in this area are a little bit suspect. Bona fide agencies will be members of one of the professional associations which will supply lists of their members on request. Government-funded small business development agencies at both national and local level can also advise on suitable agencies in your area. Informal assessments by other business people are valuable additional sources of information about the suitability or otherwise of a particular company.

Having drawn up your short-list, you might invite two or three agencies to make a presentation on how they would handle your account. You should be aware that some of them will charge you a fee for doing this. A lot of work is involved in putting together a good presentation for a prospective client, and it is only too easy for an unscrupulous operator to obtain a lot of free advice and ideas in this way. From your point of view, it is money well spent to make sure that you choose the right agency if only because the work they do on your behalf will have a major impact on your future profitability. In making your final choice, it is useful to look at each of the agencies under consideration in terms of their:

- Experience — How long have they been in business? How many clients do they have?
- Organisation — Are they efficient in the way they operate?
- Creative ability — Are you impressed by the work they have done for other clients?
- Compatibility — Have they shown themselves capable of understanding the specific needs of your business?
- General attitude — Do you think you could work with these people over a long period of time?

Finally, you should bear in mind that, although the term advertising agency has been used throughout this section, there are other types of promotional agency which may be just as suitable for your needs as a traditional advertising agency, especially in a situation where relatively little money is spent on direct media advertising. These include public relations firms, design and print consultancies, sales promotion and merchandising specialists, exhibition organisers and so on.

It is also perfectly feasible for a small firm to get by without using the services of a specialist agency. You can buy separately all the various bits and pieces you need to communicate effectively with the customer. But this will take up a lot of your time and you will have the major task of co-ordinating them into a meaningful overall promotional strategy. You can probably cope with this if your firm is very small and only a limited amount of this kind of activity is needed. But as your firm grows, more organisation and greater expertise will be required. You will eventually reach the point where it will pay you to sub-contract this task to a specialist rather than continue to do it yourself. You, and only you, can decide which is likely to be the most cost-effective approach at this particular point in your development.

Summary of Key Points
1. The main advantage of direct media advertising is that it enables you to contact a large number of potential customers at one time. Its main disadvantage is that it can be quite expensive.
2. Bear in mind that a small firm may not need to advertise at all. Direct media advertising is only one of a number of different ways of communicating with potential customers.
3. If you do decide to advertise, you need to be absolutely clear about what you are trying to achieve. You need a precise statement of your objectives, the target audience you want to reach and the message you want to convey to them. You must choose the media which will best convey your message to the maximum possible number of the right sort of people.
4. There is a straight trade-off between the number of people you can reach through a particular advertising medium and the costs involved in doing so — the bigger the audience, the higher the costs.
5. Different media have different characteristics and appeal to different people. It is important to make sure that your message is communicated through channels which fit in with the characteristics of your product or service and with the image you want to promote.

6. Advertising is essentially a creative process, requiring the imaginative use of verbal and non-verbal elements. Your advertising can be purely informative, but it should also give people a number of solid reasons why they should buy from you. This approach is called the USP (Unique Selling Proposition) method of advertising. You might also seek to develop a good brand image for your products. This can be expensive on a national scale, but it is possible for a small firm to build a sound brand image in a limited geographical area through attractive packaging, effective merchandising and some media advertising.
7. A single isolated advertisement is likely to achieve very little. Advertising is a learning process — the greater the number of repetitions, the greater the chances of your message getting through and being retained. You also need to know how effective your advertising has been. There are a number of simple techniques available to help you do this.
8. Whether or not you need to use an advertising agency depends largely on the size of your advertising budget. Many small firms do without one, but this takes up a lot of time. An advertising agency brings together all the specialist skills under one roof and can offer a level of expertise you are unlikely to have. But take care to choose an agency which you can rely on to do a good job for you.

9.
Selling

Selling is what marketing is all about. You may well be asking yourself why, then, has it taken so long to get round to it in this book. The answer is that you need to make sure all these other things are right before you can start to sell effectively. The whole point of doing market research, looking at your product and your pricing, organising effective distribution and contacting the customer through advertising and sales promotion, is to make the selling job easier.

Selling is radically different from the other ways of contacting the customer discussed in previous chapters. Advertising and sales promotion involve one-way communication — you devise your message and transmit it to your target audience through various media in the hope that they actually receive the message you intended. Sometimes it can go dreadfully wrong. For example, you may describe your product or service as 'cheap', meaning inexpensive, but your customers may interpret this in the sense of 'cheap and nasty' — i.e. badly designed and of poor quality. In contrast, the essential nature of selling is that it involves two-way communication. During a person-to-person conversation, potential customers have an opportunity to react to the proposition being offered to them. Their reaction may be non-verbal — a look, or a gesture — and the good salesperson will pick this up just as quickly as a clearly-expressed verbal objection or criticism. The message can be revised or adapted to meet and overcome their prejudices or their ignorance. That is why direct personal selling is usually the most effective way of making sure that an order is obtained. The problem is that it is also the most expensive — it takes a lot of man-hours which have to be paid for one way or another. There are several ways you can go about it. You can:

- Do it yourself.
- Employ a sales representative.
- Delegate the task to an agent or distributor.

You must have heard some of the old wives' tales about selling — that good salespeople are born and not made; you either can sell or you can't — and if you can't, there is very little you can do about it. These stories are simply not true. A more accurate way of thinking about it is to remember that the ability to sell is a bit like the ability to play golf. A few fortunate individuals are just naturally gifted and seem to be able to score consistently around par without any apparent effort. A few hopeless cases are totally devoid of natural co-ordination and will never be able to get round in under 200 strokes even if their very life depended on it. Most of us are somewhere in between these two extremes — with some instruction and a lot of practice, we can manage to achieve a fairly respectable level of performance.

All the available evidence suggests that selling is just like that. Selling skills can be learned, and with some training and a lot of practice, most people can do a reasonably effective selling job. If you are an absolute beginner, you would probably find it very useful to take a two or three-day course in selling techniques. There are plenty of them available, and you should regard the time and money you spend on it as a worthwhile investment in the future success of your business. Attending a course is often beneficial because there are so many tricks of the trade which can really only be taught by demonstrating 'live' the interaction between a good salesperson and a potential customer, and by getting the trainee sales people to try applying these techniques themselves. This is often done by simulation exercises in which the instructor (or another participant in the course) plays the role of the customer. A good sales training course will include practical demonstrations of various sales techniques by means of films, videos or role-playing, and will provide participants with feedback about their own efforts to apply them, often using closed-circuit television playback facilities. You need to make sure you choose a good course. Like everything else in this world, you can throw money down the drain buying something which looks good on paper, but does not actually deliver what it promises. One way round this problem is to ask around. Most reputable course organisers are happy enough to provide the names of previous participants who can be contacted.

To start you down the road towards becoming an expert salesperson in your own right, see if you can apply to your business the five basic steps involved in effective personal selling. These are:
- Identifying possible customers
- Arranging a meeting with them
- Making a sales presentation

- Closing the sale
- Holding on to the business

These five steps provide a logical sequence which explains what normally happens during the selling process, and it is useful to look at each of them in more detail to see what may be involved. However it is worth pointing out that every business and every customer is different, and that in some situations one or more of them may be skipped over very quickly, or left out altogether. The length of time needed to work through the whole sequence can also vary widely. It only takes a few minutes to complete a sale in a street market. In contrast, it can take months, or even years, to clinch an order for a large industrial contract.

IDENTIFYING POSSIBLE CUSTOMERS
This preliminary stage in the selling process is sometimes referred to as sales 'prospecting', a word which conjures up images of digging for gold out in the wilds somewhere. When you think about it, it is actually quite a good way of describing the task of finding customers — complex and difficult, but with the chance of a substantial financial gain if you are successful. As in the case of digging for gold, half the secret of successful sales prospecting is to know where to look in the first place. You need to start by doing some research, going right back to the fundamentals of marketing.

- Who buys this kind of product or service?
- How, when, where, how often and how much do they buy?
- What factors influence their choice?

What you do next depends on your answers to these basic questions. For some types of business, the most effective way forward is to generate a steady flow of enquiries from the general public through appropriate advertising and sales promotions. For example, many small firms in the building trade tap into the ongoing need of householders for basic maintenance services (painting and decorating, plumbing, roofing, electrical work, replacement windows and so on) by more or less continuous advertising at a highly local level.

Services
The same basic strategy is adopted by firms providing personal services of one kind or another which require the customer to come to them, rather than the other way round (for example hairdressers, car repairs, replacement tyres, batteries and exhaust systems). The only difference is that, in this case, the more efficient operators also pay a great deal of

attention to attracting a passing trade. They do this primarily by choosing the best possible site to begin with, and then making sure that it is well signposted so that nobody could possibly miss it. It then becomes a question of organising an effective follow-up which will turn as high a proportion as possible of the enquiries received into actual orders. This involves taking care to ensure that every enquirer, either by telephone or in person, is dealt with politely and promptly, and that accurate information is provided on what is available. It is also often essential that some additional information about the enquirer is recorded accurately — most typically his or her name, address and telephone number. This is all very elementary advice — but you would be amazed to discover how many small firms lose a lot of business by failing to heed it. Just pause for a moment and reflect. Are you absolutely certain that every enquiry your firm receives from a potential customer is handled in a way which maximises your chances of obtaining their business?

The behaviour of firms which operate in this way is better described by the example of a fishing boat, rather than a prospector for rare precious metals. In effect what they do is to trawl through the great mass of potential customers at regular intervals in the hope of catching enough of them in the net to keep the business profitable. This approach works well in situations where you are selling direct to the general public. It is much less efficient when 'the customer' is another organisation — a supermarket chain, or another company or a government department. In these cases a lot more digging is required.

Selling to large organisations

If you know your own particular industry well, you will probably already be able to draw up a list of the most important potential customers. On the other hand, you may need to start compiling the list virtually from scratch. This will involve collecting information from a wide range of sources, including:

- Personal contacts, in the trade
- Personal observation
- Trade and technical journals
- Directories
- Your own existing customers

In either case, the absolute minimum information requirement is to identify as far as possible:

- Which products/services are they most likely to buy from you?
- Who is the right person to see?

- Who is supplying these products/services at present?
- On what terms?

All of this seems a bit of a tall order, but you will be surprised at how much valuable information you will be able to uncover fairly easily. Reading 'between the lines' in the trade press will provide useful hints and provide indications of who is doing business with whom. You can build up a comprehensive dossier on who is supplying a particular product to a supermarket chain simply by walking round one of their branches. Finding out the detailed terms that have been negotiated is rather more difficult, but by no means impossible. Many people in business are more than willing to display their knowledge of who's who and what's what, and indeed are often quite flattered when they are presented with an opportunity to do so. Don't be afraid to ask questions along the lines of:

- Who is the right person to talk to?
- What kind of person are they?
- What is the best time to get hold of the person?

The need for good records

Storing all this valuable information for future use is not a problem today. Almost every standard personal computer provides a basic data storage and retrieval system and it is not especially difficult to set up an appropriate spreadsheet. Even if you do not have a PC at your disposal, you can still devise a manual recording system appropriate to your needs. The one thing you should *not* do is to rely entirely on your own memory — you have quite enough to think about already.

Once you have built up a good data-base of market intelligence along these lines, you should go through it carefully and make an assessment of what you have discovered about each potential customer's requirements and about the activities of your competitors. You also need to bear in mind your own limitations and capabilities as a potential supplier. You will find it helpful to give each of them a rating in terms of your chances of persuading them to do business with you. Your rating system need not be very complicated — a simple grading of potential customers as A, B or C prospects would suffice. Selling takes a lot of time and effort, and it makes sense to target your efforts on where you are most likely to succeed rather than to waste it in no-hope situations.

Former customers

One group of potential future customers you should not overlook is the people with whom you have done business in the past but have since lost for one reason or another. You should keep a record of former customers and go back to it from time to time. Remember that things change in business as in every other walk of life, sometimes very rapidly. You may well discover, for example, that the competitor who forced you out by undercutting you is now trying to raise his/her price, thus giving you an opportunity to bid for the order again. Or your competitors may be finding that the only way they can stay in business at the lower price they quoted is by cutting back on quality, with the result that the customer is now prepared to pay a bit more for a better product or service. It often pays dividends to ask yourself in respect of each former customer:

- Why did we lose them?
- How can we get them back again?

MEETING POTENTIAL CUSTOMERS

It is not usually a good idea to arrive unannounced on the customer's doorstep. Put yourself in that position and it is easy to see why it is nearly always better to make a firm appointment. Imagine you are busy doing something you really should have got out of the way at least a week ago and your secretary announces that some character sitting in the outside office wants to see you — now! Your most likely reaction is to tell your visitor to get lost. Even if you agree to see him or her because you are basically a nice person, the chances are you will get rid of them as soon as you possibly can and you will only be half listening to what has been said. Attempting to sell in this way is sometimes referred to as 'cold calling'.

The same sort of scenario applies to situations where you need to call at someone's home in response to an initial enquiry — for example to measure up for replacement windows, or do a survey for an electrical rewiring job. You will not be well received if the lady of the house is cooking dinner or putting the children to bed. You will have completely wasted your time if she happens to be out shopping when you choose to call. It is much more sensible to arrange a meeting at a time which is convenient both for you and for the customer. Whether you do this by letter or telephone depends on the circumstances, but you need to make sure that you will see the right person — i.e. the person who has the authority to give the order. There is no point in allowing yourself to be diverted to a second or third choice, so that you end up spending an hour or so making your presentation, only to be told that the person you have been talking to is not in a position to make a decision.

This in fact emphasises the need for some previous research, because it assumes that you actually know who the right person is. That kind of knowledge is often vital in the sometimes tricky process of setting up a meeting. You are much more likely to be successful if you ask to speak to a named person rather than simply 'the works manager' or 'the chief buyer'. In any event, you should not expect to be received with open arms. Many people regard seeing a sales rep as a total pain in the neck. But do not give up too easily. Patience and persistence are essential attributes of the successful sales person.

MAKING A SALES PRESENTATION

It is naive and unrealistic to think that you can simply breeze into a meeting with a possible customer, overwhelm him or her with your natural charm and come out ten minutes later with a huge order signed and sealed and safely in your inside pocket. It is just not like that in the real world. Before you go anywhere near the customer, it is essential that you apply the old Boy Scouts' motto — be prepared. Detailed preparation well in advance of the actual meeting is essential for successful selling. You need to:

- Set your objectives.
- Think out your approach.
- Prepare a sales kit.

Setting Objectives

Your ultimate objective is, of course, to make a sale. But you must accept the fact that several meetings may be required before you reach that point. You need to be flexible and realistic in your approach, and think out what alternatives you would by happy with, short of actually taking a firm order. You need to bear in mind the thought process your customers go through, from when they know little or nothing about you and your product to the point at which they decide to place an order with you. There are a number of separate steps involved in the development of their thinking:

- attracting their attention
- arousing their interest
- deciding that they want to buy
- taking positive action to do so

If you apply that sequence of thought to your contacts with a particular customer, you may decide that the basic purpose of your first meeting may be simply to create awareness and arouse interest, with the desired outcome being a firm appointment for a second meeting. Failing that, your fall-back position might be to leave samples and a sales catalogue with a customer and find out when might be the best time to contact him or her again. If you are going in with the objective of obtaining a firm order, but it becomes apparent during the interview that you are unlikely to succeed, your fall-back alternative might be to arrange a demonstration on the customer's premises, or to persuade him or her to accept some samples, or perhaps even give you a small trial order 'to see how it goes'.

There is an enormously wide range of possible primary and alternative objectives for different products and different customers. You will have to work out the detail of these alternatives for yourself in relation to your own particular circumstances. But the basic point still holds — you need to set your objectives in advance of meeting with the customer, and you need to be flexible enough to allow for the possibility that you will not always achieve them first time round.

Deciding on your approach

Setting realistic objectives is an important aspect of thinking through your overall approach, but you also need to work out in some detail what you are going to say and how you are going to say it. A key element in this is the information you have managed to acquire about the person you are going to see. You need to have a fairly precise knowledge of their likely needs in terms of the products and services you can provide, and of how these needs are being met at present — in other words, which of your competitors is currently supplying them. But it is also very helpful to find out as much as you can about potential buyers as people — their likes and dislikes, prejudices, interests, social and family background and so on. This kind of information is of tremendous value in helping you to establish a personal rapport with your client, which is vitally important if you are to succeed in obtaining his business.

The way in which you handle this aspect of your sales presentation will obviously vary, since every customer is different, but you also need to work out a general framework which you can apply to most situations. The notion that you should work out a standard sales patter which you use on every occasion is a bit 'old hat' nowadays, mainly because that kind of approach is not particularly effective. The sales message you are trying to get across needs to be adapted and presented in a way which takes account of the varying needs and personalities of different customers. But it is still possible to work out in advance a broad line of approach on which each individual presentation will be based. To do this effectively, you need to:

- emphasise the benefits
- anticipate the objections

Benefits

A clear presentation of the benefits the customer will derive from doing business with you lies at the heart of any successful sales meeting. It is well worth the time and effort involved in drawing up a comprehensive list of what your product or service can offer. But you must remember to emphasise the benefits to the customer, not simply the features of the product. To illustrate the point, it may not be all that interesting to the customer that a new machine incorporates a particular type of electrical motor with a trip-out device to avoid overloading (i.e. a product feature). The customer will be much more interested to hear that running and maintenance costs are twenty per cent lower than the machine he or she is currently using and that lost production through breakdowns as a result of overloading can be virtually eliminated (benefits to the customer). Again, a bemused housewife recently emerged from a car showroom having listened to an enthusiastic young salesman's lecture which included references to brake horse power, torque and catalytic convertors. She was heard to remark: 'I only wanted to know if it could run on lead-free petrol'.

Objections

With a bit of thought, you can also anticipate the kind of objections customers will bring up. You can then work out in advance how you are going to deal with them. This is not as easy as it sounds, and you will have to put a lot of thought into how best to overcome these objections. As a general rule, the best way to go about it is to put the objection into perspective in terms of the total deal that you are offering, and if possible immediately offer some other kind of benefit as a compensation. For example, if a customer suggests that your product is too expensive (which is far and away the most common objection you will encounter), an effective way of overcoming his or her doubts might be to point out that your product is of much better quality and will therefore last longer. Over a five year period, the potential buyer would have to buy only two sets of your product as compared with five or six sets of the (apparently) cheaper alternative. Here again, every product and service is different. You will have to apply the notion of anticipating and overcoming objections in a way which is appropriate to your own operation.

Preparing a sales kit

You would no doubt take a very dim view of an employee who went off to do an installation job without a tool kit, on the very sensible grounds that it is impossible to do the job properly without one. The same thinking applies to the task of selling. A suitable tool kit is needed to make an effective sales presentation. You need to answer two questions before you decide what your selling kit should contain.

- What are you going to show the customer?
- What are you going to leave with the customer?

Your answer to the first of these questions may well be 'nothing' — but if that is the case, you will need to think again. There is a lot of truth in the old saying that a picture is worth a thousand words. It is so much simpler to be able to say to the customer 'this is what I mean', rather than gabbling on and on about it. Good sales aids are a useful way of getting the customer's attention and stimulating his or her interest. For a small firm, this usually involves preparing:

- samples
- a sales manual

Samples

It is often possible to show the customer samples of the actual product itself. But even when the finished product is too bulky for this to be feasible, it is usually not too difficult to come up with a meaningful sample. You will no doubt have come across those 'books' of wallpaper or carpet samples or the collections of small pieces of cloth which are sometimes used to help you choose the material for a new suit. The same principle can be applied in many other areas — pieces of wood, metal or plastic perhaps with different finishes. Small machined parts could show the design and quality of the work you produce. A printing firm can easily assemble a collection of different kinds of work previously undertaken for other customers. Plans, photographs, drawings and perhaps even a small-scale model of the finished article are better than relying on words alone.

But you should remember that poor samples can be counter-productive. You need to keep them up-to-date, and change them regularly when they show signs of becoming a little bit tatty through constant use. A video can be a very effective way of showing prospective customers your premises and your products in action. Since many customers will not have a video recorder available on the premises, you will often need to take portable equipment with you on sales visits. Just remember that the basic rule for any kind of publicity material also applies to a video — it has to be of good quality. A half-baked, amateurish effort is quite likely to be counter-productive in the impression it creates. At present, you would need to spend a minimum of about £5000 to produce a good one.

Sales manual

A sales manual is simply a handy way of keeping your brochures, leaflets, price lists and other sales aids together, and of using them in a structured way as the focus of your presentation. It usually consists of a loose-leaf binder which you can go through with the customer, explaining each point you wish to bring out, perhaps re-inforcing it with an illustration. Some salespeople find it useful to include not only their own sales literature but also additional material which helps to back up their case. This might include, for example, a letter from a government department appointing you as an approved supplier or testimonials from satisfied customers.

Your customers are not likely to remember everything you have said to them during your presentation. They may also need to consult with someone else before making a final decision. It is important to leave something with them which will, in a sense, go on selling after you have left. Leaving them your samples can provide a legitimate reason for calling back again, but this has the disadvantage that you will go through a lot of samples, which can be expensive. The alternative is to give them some of your sales literature — your brochure or catalogue, price lists and technical data sheets. As an absolute minimum, you need to make sure they have your name and telephone number so that they can contact you if they wish to do so. A simple business card is sufficient for this purpose.

Talking to the customer

Even though you have done all your homework in advance, your performance during your face-to-face encounter with the customer will determine how far you progress towards making a sale. The only way to improve is by practice, and by learning from your mistakes. But there are some key points which you may find helpful. During a sales presentation you should try to do a number of essential things.

- Keep calm and in control.
- Emphasise the benefits, not the features.
- Ask questions.
- Overcome objections.
- Ask for the order.

It is a major mistake to appear to be so laid back that you are in danger of falling over, but it is equally important to keep cool no matter what happens. Your attitude throughout should be friendly and direct. You should not argue or become emotionally involved, even when the buyer seems to be deliberately trying to knock you out of your stride by being off-handed or downright rude. You should try to keep control of what is happening, in the sense of not allowing yourself to be diverted or side-tracked away from the main object of the exercise.

Do not be afraid to ask questions, but make sure you phrase them in such a way that it is difficult for the other person to give you a simple 'Yes' or 'No' answer. For example, instead of asking someone 'Are maintenance costs important to you?', you might ask 'What level of maintenance costs would you expect for a machine of this kind?'. Putting the question this way will provide you with extra information on which you can build; it is very difficult to build anything on a blunt 'Yes' or 'No'.

Another useful technique for keeping control is to reply to a question with a question. For example, if someone asks: 'Why is your product so expensive?', you might counter by asking: 'What makes you say that?' Their reply will probably give you some useful information about their current supplier, or will tell you who else they have contacted.

When you are presented with objections of one kind or another, try to make them as specific as possible so that you can respond to them effectively. For instance, a supermarket buyer might object that the shelf-life of the product you are offering is not long enough. You might respond to this by asking how many days of shelf-life are required for products of this kind. Hopefully you will be able to point out that you can work within these parameters if that is what is needed. Finally, you need to be sensitive in choosing the right moment to ask for the order.

CLOSING THE SALE

The first thing you have to accept is that you may not be able to close the sale (i.e. obtain an order) — at least not this time. Even though you have convinced the customer to buy, you may discover that he or she is not prepared to do so at present for any number of reasons. It may be the wrong time of year, the budget may be used up, someone else's approval may be required, or whatever. In these situations, it is of paramount importance to discover when is the best time to try again. Too many small firms make the mistake of giving up too easily, assuming that doors have been closed finally and irrevocably because the first attempt was unsuccessful.

If you decide that you are in with a good chance of getting an order there and then, you need to gently nudge the customer to the point where a firm undertaking to purchase is given. You need to watch out for 'buying signals' — hints from the customer that what you are proposing is satisfactory. These signals may be quite clear, as when a customer starts asking detailed questions about when you could arrange delivery. More usually, you have to rely on close observation of what the customer is saying and doing in order to pick up the clues. You might find it useful to try and bring the proceedings to a successful conclusion by beginning to talk in terms which assume that an order will be placed. 'Which colours would you like?' or 'Do you want me to arrange deliveries twice a week, or is every Thursday morning OK?' If you get positive answers to these kind of questions, you are more or less home and dry. But you may finally have to politely ask for the order in a more direct way.

Remember too that in some circumstances, it is essential to follow up the administrative procedures involved. In many big companies and government departments, it is normal procedure for an order to be issued by someone other than the person to whom you have been talking. You have not finally closed the sale until that piece of paper confirming the order has arrived safely in your in-tray. Some other kinds of business require the provision of detailed specifications and an exchange of draft contracts before an order is confirmed. You have not closed the sale until this has been done.

HOLDING ON TO THE BUSINESS
In most selling situations, you should not be aiming for a one-off sale. You should be trying to establish a continuing relationship with customers who will give you repeat orders for quite a long period of time. Their experience of how you handle the initial order is of critical importance in determining whether or not you succeed in obtaining repeats. You need to make absolutely certain that your company's performance lives up to the promises you have made, that delivery dates are met and so on. This will involve contacting the customer again to make sure that everything is satisfactory and taking prompt remedial action if there are any problems. You also need to maintain regular contact with the customer to find out when repeat orders are likely to arise. You cannot simply assume that from here on, the customer will come to you.

Summary of Key Points
1. Selling skills can be learned. With some training and a lot of practice, most people can do a reasonably effective selling job. The key tasks involved are identifying possible customers and making a sales presentation to them.

2. Prospecting for sales leads involves a lot of basic research — there is no easy way. You should not be discouraged if you fail to get an order on your first visit to a potential new customer — keep at it. You need to think carefully through your sales approach, identifying the customer benefits to highlight, and the objections you may encounter.
3. Some kind of sales kit is essential for a good sales presentation. This will usually comprise at the minimum a file containing brochures and price list, together with samples and other sales aids which might be useful.
4. There is a technique involved in giving a good sales presentation. You should aim to keep calm and in control of the interview, ask open questions, overcome objections and ask for an order.
5. In most selling situations, you are not looking for a one-off sale. You should be trying to establish a relationship which will generate a flow of repeat orders. To achieve this, it is essential that the order is actually delivered on time and according to specification.

10.
Sales Management

As your business expands, sooner or later you will reach the point where it is no longer physically possible for you to follow up all the sales leads that are being generated. You will find that you are having to work excessively long hours, including evenings and weekends. You are quite likely to become over-tired, so that other aspects of running the business begin to suffer. At that point, you will have to think seriously about what is involved in employing someone else to do at least part of the selling job for you. If you insist on trying to do it all yourself, the chances are you will end up having a heart attack, or developing an ulcer — or both, if you really work at it. Alternatively, you may have decided within the context of a carefully worked-out expansion plan that you will need to increase your sales volume substantially. To pay for the larger premises, new plant and machinery, extra staff and so on which are required to achieve a specific profit target, you will have to raise your turnover by, say, twenty per cent a year over the next three years — and the only way you can ever hope to do that is by employing a salesperson. Incidentally you may have noticed that throughout this book the terms 'salesperson' or 'salespeople' have been used, rather than the more traditional 'salesman'. This has been done deliberately, for two reasons. First, it recognises the fact that more and more women are now being employed in selling jobs. Secondly, it reminds you that many women are out-performing their male colleagues in that role. Some experts would go as far as to argue that women are actually more likely than men to be good at selling, because women in general are much better at picking up the verbal and non-verbal signals which are so important in face-to-face communication.

However you need to do your sums very carefully before going down this particular road. Bringing a specialist salesperson on board is a very big step indeed for a small firm. As a very rough guide, in Ireland at the present time you can reckon it will cost you a minimum of about £25,000 a year. That figure includes basic salary and commission, statutory payments of one kind or another, subsistence and entertainment expenses and the costs of providing transport. Think about it for a minute or two. If you are operating on a twenty per cent profit margin, then your sales rep will have to bring in an additional £125,000 worth of orders before you break even. You will achieve a net gain in company profitability only when he or she does better than that. You can do the appropriate calculation for your own firm along these lines.

Whatever answer you come up with, the basic point is still relevant — you need to be clear about what you are letting yourself in for before you start drafting an advert for the 'Situations Vacant' column of your local paper. Nevertheless, the hard realities of running a business in this day and age will eventually bring you back to the point where you have to face up to the critical decision. You simply cannot do it all yourself. If you want to expand, sooner or later you will have to employ sales staff. When you arrive at this stage of your company's development, it is of crucial importance to do a preliminary check to make sure that the extra business is actually there. You will also be faced with a whole new set of management tasks which will soon become problems if you have no idea how to handle them. These include:

- Recruitment
- Training
- Remuneration
- Motivation
- Organisation and control

RECRUITMENT

It is hardly worth taking the trouble to remind you how vitally important it is to recruit the best possible person for the job. After all, you are in a very real sense entrusting the future of your business to that person. However finding the right person presupposes that you have a clear idea of what you are looking for. Before you go any further, you need to think carefully through a number of issues which a management consultant would describe as 'carrying out a job analysis'. These include the following.

- What kind of technical knowledge is required?
- What kind of local or customer knowledge is required?
- What specific tasks do you want your salesperson to undertake?

Some kinds of selling jobs demand a high level of technical expertise and can really only be done by a suitably qualified person such as an engineer. In other situations, it is fairly easy to pick up a detailed knowledge of customer needs and product attributes, so that what you are looking for is someone with good selling skills, perhaps learned in a completely different kind of business. Then again, it might be very important that your sales rep is familiar with the attitudes and behaviour patterns of a particular target group of customers — e.g. farmers or hospital administrators. The basic task of the sales person is, of course, to obtain orders from customers. But there are many different ways of going about that task and many different skills are required. You need to sort out what specific tasks your sales people will need to be able to perform. These may include:

- making appointments by telephone
- writing letters
- preparing detailed quotations
- meeting customers in their own home
- negotiating with senior executives
- handling paperwork
- merchandising and display
- arranging exhibitions and demonstrations
- giving technical advice

The person you employ will have to be able to do at least some of these things, but probably not all of them. You need to be clear in your own mind what kind of sales person you require. You then need to develop your job analysis into a detailed job description. You will need this to help you select the most suitable candidate from the possibly large number of applications you will receive if you advertise the post. You will also need to give a copy of it to the person you appoint so that both of you are clear about what the job entails right from day one.

Finding suitable staff

Only when you have done a job analysis and written a job description will you be ready to go out looking for the right person. You may not need to go outside the company at all. There may well be an existing employee who could make a suitable sales representative with appropriate training. The advantages of using an existing employee are that they already know your business well, and you can be sure that you can rely on them rather than taking on an unknown quantity. You may also come across someone suitable as a result of informal contact with other people in business. For instance, if a competitor has ceased trading, you can be fairly certain that there will be one or two experienced people looking for a job. You may also be able to attract someone from a competing firm by offering them a better deal. This has the advantage that you will also acquire that person's contacts — but you need to be wary of this kind of 'poaching' which can sometimes lead to a very messy succession of short-term appointments as different firms try to out-bid each other.

If you decide to advertise the post, you will need to devise some way to enable applicants to tell you about what they have to offer. Most small firms do not have a standard application form, and it is scarcely worth the effort involved in drawing one up since you are not going to be appointing people all that often. It is usually sufficient to invite applicants to send you a full curriculum vitae. You will then have to draw up a short list and interview those who seem suitable. The CVs will tell you a great deal about the quality of different applicants other than the basic facts of their age, qualifications, experience to date and previous employment history. Someone who tries to sell himself/herself by providing a barely legible, incoherent CV written on a page torn out of a child's exercise book is hardly likely to do a good job selling your product.

Interviewing applicants

Interviewing people for a sales job is not quite as straightforward as it might seem. The problem is that virtually anyone can put on a good show for half an hour or so. What you are trying to discover is how they would handle a bad-tempered customer at the end of a long day. There are some basic attributes that good sales representatives should have. They should turn up on time, be neatly dressed and reasonably articulate. But it is quite wrong to assume that a sales representative needs to be a loud-mouthed extrovert with an inexhaustible fund of dubious stories. The essential quality you are looking for is sometimes referred to as 'empathy' — the ability to be sensitive to and adapt to the personality of the other party involved. You may have noticed how a good sales rep treats every customer in a slightly different way, and somehow manages to establish a rapport with even the most difficult of them. Another essential quality is the self-discipline and drive needed to cope with a job which is often lonely and stressful and where direct day-to-day supervision is not possible. Many big firms have devised psychological tests designed to find out to what extent applicants for sales posts possess these desirable attributes. That is a luxury you are most unlikely to be able to afford. You will have to rely largely on your own judgment based on performance during the interview, but you should always try and obtain a second opinion where possible. Before you offer someone the job, you should take the trouble to contact the people he or she has nominated as being willing to provide a reference. It is also sometimes useful to contact their previous employer to obtain a different perspective on the person you are considering — there are always two sides to every story.

TRAINING

Regardless of how much experience your new salesperson may have acquired, he or she will need some sort of initial training if they are to do an effective job for you. Before you send them out on their own they need to have a full briefing on:

- your products
- your customers
- your competitors
- company policies and procedures

A salesperson needs full and detailed knowledge of all possible uses of every product, their prices, styles, likely new developments and so on. You will need to provide whatever information you have about your customers' needs, motives and buying patterns. You will also be able to provide useful hints on how to make an effective sales presentation — which major selling 'themes' work best based on your own past experience and on how these should be presented in various different situations. A sales rep also needs to know about the opposition — their product lines and how they compare with your own; their policies on credit, delivery charges, after sales service and so on. Finally, the salesperson must identify with the company and be familiar with its administrative procedures for ordering, reporting, registering complaints, obtaining expenses and the like.

The amount of training required depends on how experienced your new salesperson is. An old hand would obviously need a lot less than a new recruit fresh from college. Just remember that if you send out raw recruits with a few samples, a pile of leaflets and a list of names and addresses, they are more likely to sink than swim. In the early stages, they should accompany you on your sales calls to learn what selling themes and approaches can be used and how these need to be adapted to different customers. You can also show them, for example, how best to arrange meetings using the telephone and how to organise their appointments to minimise travelling time. Finally, remember that the need for training is on-going. It is not something you can deal with in the first couple of weeks and then forget about. Bad habits can be acquired; products, policies and procedures changed. You will need to bring your sales people up to date at regular intervals.

REMUNERATION

If you are to have any chance of recruiting decent sales staff and of holding on to them, it is crucial that you offer the right level of remuneration. However, having said that, a tremendous variety of different remuneration packages has been devised, and about the only thing that can be said with absolute certainty is that there are no hard and fast rules for establishing which of them is correct. The problem arises primarily because of the need to reconcile the different and sometimes conflicting objectives of managers and employees. From a management point of view, the deal offered to sales staff must be structured to provide a measure of:

- Economy
- Simplicity
- Flexibility
- Control

The basic requirement is that the total costs of your sales staff must be in line with the revenue they generate; otherwise you will soon be in trouble. This will involve doing some calculations to establish the volume of sales needed at your current (or anticipated) profit levels to earn a reasonable return on your outlay. You would be wise to seek the advice of your accountant on this point. Some large firms operate very complex schemes, with different rates of commission payable on different products and with variations in commission rates as successively higher sales targets are achieved.

The remuneration package you devise must be simple to understand and administer. Otherwise you will be involved in endless disputes with your sales staff and you will incur substantial additional clerical costs in working out how much is due to each of them at the end of the month. It must also be flexible, in the sense that it can be adapted easily to changing circumstances. Major problems can arise from being locked into a particular system. Finally, a flexible remuneration package is one of the ways in which management can control the activities of the sales force. If greater effort is needed in a particular area, say to launch a new product or enter a new area, this can often be encouraged by offering appropriate rewards, financial or otherwise.

From the point of view of the sales person, the basic requirements are likely to be:

- a guaranteed regular basic income
- additional payments related to performance
- equity

Sales Management

Selling is by definition a fairly risky occupation. In this day and age, very few people are prepared to accept the risk of a nil income if sales are poor due to factors outside their control. Remuneration on a commission-only basis is now quite a rarity. Most sales people expect to earn more for better than average performance, but here again there are many different ways of putting this principle into practice.

Performance-related remuneration

The simplest approach is to pay a fairly low basic salary which is topped up by commission (i.e. an additional payment based on total sales). This system has the advantage of being easy to administer, but it also suffers from some disadvantages. You need to clarify when exactly the commission payment is due. On receipt of the order? Or only when the customer finally pays up? Again, disputes often arise in situations where it is not clear which person actually obtained the order. For instance, you may have made an initial contact which is followed up by a sales rep. Is the sales person entitled to full commission on that sale? Or only a proportion of it? And if so, what proportion? Another disadvantage with this approach is that your sales staff may switch off their efforts once they have reached what they consider to be an adequate income for the month. They will in effect trade-off higher wages for additional leisure time.

One way round this is to pay commission only on sales above an agreed target level. A further possible refinement is to add the incentive of a lump-sum bonus on top of basic salary and commission if a specified high volume of sales is achieved. The question then arises of what are the appropriate levels above which commission and bonus payments are made. This is best decided by detailed discussion between the manager and the sales people, taking account of the potential business likely to be available and of any special problems likely to be encountered. The existing customer base should be reviewed account by account and estimates made of the prospects of obtaining repeat and additional orders. An estimate of possible new business can then be added to produce an agreed target. It is usually counter-productive to simply impose a sales target without consultations of this kind. If the sales people believe that the targets set for them are impossibly high, they will mentally readjust them to what they consider to be more attainable levels (while possibly looking round for another job at the same time). In contrast, a sales person will feel much more personally committed to achieving a target which he or she has had a hand in setting.

Equity

The idea of equity in terms of remuneration simply means that sales people, indeed every employee, will expect fair treatment as compared with other employees in the same company, with employees doing the same job in other companies, and with the cost of living. Their performance is bound to suffer if they believe otherwise. You need to find out what is the going rate for a sales person in your particular industry and make sure that you offer somewhere close to that average level. You will have major recruitment problems if you pitch it too low. Remember the old saying — if you pay peanuts, you only attract monkeys. Alternatively, you may be increasing your overheads unnecessarily if you go too high. You also need to bear in mind that sales people tend to think in terms of the overall remuneration package offered, which is made up of four separate elements.

- Basic salary
- Additional performance-related payments
- Fringe benefits
- Expenses

The agreed basic salary must be sufficient to provide a stable regular income to feed the family and pay the mortgage. But the real icing on the cake comes from the additional payments on offer. These can take many forms other than commission or bonuses, for example profit-sharing. They can also be non-monetary. For example, the bonus may take the form of a 'free' holiday or a set of golf clubs. However, the most important fringe benefit most sales people take into account is the quality of the company car provided. Entitlement to travel, subsistence and entertainment expenses may be generous or miserly. But there is no doubt that many sales people regard the quality of the car they drive and the hotel they stay in as clear reflections of their status and in a sense a part of their overall remuneration package.

MOTIVATION

People work because they need money, but it is quite wrong to think that financial rewards are the only way to motivate people. Your employees must be more or less content that what they take home in their pay-packet is a reasonable return for the efforts they have made on your behalf. It is absolutely certain that they will be totally de-motivated if this basic expectation is not fulfilled. But that does not mean to say they will always pull out all the stops for you simply because you are paying them adequately. Sales people in particular often need a lot of extra motivation because of the stressful nature of the job. They have to work long irregular hours and are frequently away from home. They have to work at the front line of the battle with the competition — every sales person is only too aware that an order they have worked hard to win can be lost at the very last minute. If the opposition has not contacted the customer yesterday, there is a fair chance they will do so tomorrow. Every sales person is also aware that the customer ultimately calls the shots. There are many occasions where the seller has to bite his or her tongue and keep their cool (at least superficially) simply because the buyer has the power to give or withhold an order. Sales people work alone and do not have the benefit of sharing the frustrations of the job with colleagues, as most employees do from time to time. If an order is lost, salespeople must pick themselves up, dust themselves off, and start all over again. For all of these reasons, you need to take positive steps to maintain the motivation of your salespeople at a high level. Sales targets, commission and bonus payments and fringe benefits play an important role in this, but you should also provide:

- regular feedback on performance
- encouragement and support
- recognition of their efforts

Many small firms hold a sales meeting every Monday morning or Friday afternoon, according to taste. The primary purpose of these meetings is to report progress during the previous week, exchange information on new developments and organise for the week ahead. This is essential to sound management of the sales team's activities. Regular meetings are also important in terms of giving the salespeople an opportunity to share experiences and let off steam. If a sales rep has had a particularly bad week, it is enormously reassuring to discover that everyone else has also suffered. Conversely, if everyone else has done well, this provides a substantial stimulus to improve an individual's performance in the weeks ahead.

Incidentally, if a salesperson is finding the going particularly hard, the *last* thing you should do is to aggressively pressurise him or her. They will *know* when things are not going too well — you don't need to tell them. A more productive approach is to calmly and objectively review what they have been doing, trying to discover where they have been going wrong and working out how to put it right. Threatening people with the sack because things are going badly is usually counterproductive. It might come to that in the end — but they know that as well as you do.

The way in which sales people are regarded by their fellow employees is also an important motivator. Are they tolerated as a necessary evil, or are they highly thought of as people who make a vitally important contribution to the firm's overall success? Do production staff regard any suggestions or requests they may make as undesirable interference, or as a positive attempt to improve overall efficiency? You should aim to create an organisational climate in which your sales staff are given the recognition and esteem they need. You should also not hesitate to dish out praise when it is merited. Most people respond very positively if it is made clear that good performance is appreciated.

ORGANISATION AND CONTROL

It has been estimated that, on average, sales people actually sell for only about two and a half hours out of a typical eight-hour day. A lot of time is taken up in other activities, including:

- arranging appointments
- travelling to them
- finding the customer's premises
- waiting in reception
- engaging in polite conversation before getting down to business

Against that background, it is easy to see why it is essential to organise things so that you make the most effective use of their valuable time. Even if you employ only a single salesperson, you need to think about how you are going to control what is happening out there on a day-to-day basis. To do this effectively, you will need to:

- define sales territories
- decide how best to cover them
- set sales targets
- hold regular meetings
- keep accurate records
- evaluate performance

Defining sales territories

No doubt you already have a fairly clear idea of the geographical area which you are going to try and service. What you need to do now is to divide that area up into manageable territories. For instance, you might sub-divide the Greater Dublin area into four parts — Central, North, West and South. The purpose of this is to enable you to organise your coverage of customers in a planned and systematic way. The details of how you do this will depend on how many sales people you have available. If you do not employ any sales staff so that you have to do all the selling yourself, you might operate to a four-weekly cycle, devoting a week to each territory in turn. You could use a single salesperson in the same way or allocate a separate territory to each salesperson if you have more than one available.

Taking a slightly different approach, you might identify your 'key accounts' (i.e. your most important customers) and treat them as a separate 'territory' which you handle yourself, leaving the sales people to cover the rest. You might decide that, for your particular business, it is better to define the 'territories' in terms of different kinds of customers rather than as geographical areas. For instance, a firm selling catering equipment might regard industrial caterers (factories and offices), institutional caterers (hospitals, schools and so on) and the hotel trade as separate territories. The key point is to allocate clear areas of responsibility for each person involved in the selling effort.

Ensuring adequate coverage
To help you decide how best to cover the sales territories you have defined, you will need to work out as best you can:

- the total number of sales calls it is feasible for your sales staff to make in a given period;
- the total number of sales calls likely to be required over the same period.

The basic problem you have to resolve is that, while there is a finite limit on the number of calls possible, there is no limitation on the total number of calls it might be worth making. Based on your own experience, you may come to the conclusion that in your sort of business, a salesperson can only be expected to make, say, six calls a day, i.e. thirty a week. Looking at it from the other side of the coin, you might decide that each of your 100 existing customers needs a sales visit once a month. No problem — that works out at a requirement for twenty-five sales visits a week, leaving a bit of spare capacity for following up new sales leads. However, if you have 160 customers each requiring a monthly visit, or alternatively eighty customers who need to be visited once a fortnight, then you have a big problem. In that situation your alternatives are:

- call less frequently with some, or all, of your customers
- require your sales staff to make more calls
- reduce the number of customers you deal with
- increase the number of sales staff you employ

Sometimes you can reduce the number of sales visits required by contacting some customers by telephone, but this is usually possible only where you have built up a solid relationship with them which is not under immediate threat from your competitors. For instance you might call to a customer once every six weeks rather than once a month, taking repeat orders by phone every second and fourth week. You might pressurise your sales staff by increasing their work-load, but at some point this will become counter-productive. The option of sacrificing potential business by reducing the total number of customers you service is not usually a good idea. Just occasionally, you might conclude that the amount of business you are getting from a particular account is simply not worth the time and expense involved. You may well come to the rather depressing conclusion that there is a lot more business out there which you could get hold of if only you could afford to hire another salesperson to go after it, but that this is not a viable option at present. The key point is that you need to do an analysis along these lines, balancing what is desirable against what is possible. Here again, every business will be different and there are unfortunately no simple answers that can be applied in every situation.

Setting sales targets
Setting sales targets is a useful way of motivating your sales staff, provided that the targets are reasonable and attainable. The need to work out targets in consultation with them has already been noted. However targets are also a useful tool for management control purposes. If you have no measure of what is supposed to be happening, then you have no way of keeping track of whether things are going well or badly. Progress can be monitored by holding regular meetings with your sales staff, during which you can receive verbal reports from them and redirect their efforts if necessary.

Keeping sales records
Some kind of system for keeping an accurate record of your sales is also essential. You will of course have procedures for taking orders, fulfilling them and invoicing the customer. From these internal records it is relatively easy to keep a running total of sales to date for the current year by product and area. However, if you run the kind of business which depends on repeat orders from an established group of customers, you will also find it useful to have your sales people keep a record of their relationship with each customer. This may consist of a simple card index giving essential basic information. There are two reasons why this is necessary. First, even the best sales people do not have total recall, and it is often very helpful if they are able to refresh their memory about a particular customer before making a sales call. Secondly, if a

sales person should leave, a decent set of customer records will make it much easier for a replacement to take over. Many big companies also require their sales staff to write a weekly record on their activities, giving details of:
- the number of calls made
- the value of orders taken
- any other useful information they have picked up

In the smaller firm, it may not be necessary to go as far as to require a written report along these lines. Verbal reports are usually sufficient.

Evaluating performance

Finally you need to evaluate the performance of your sales staff in some way. This can be done on the basis of:
- person-to-person comparisons, *or*
- comparisons of current to past performance

Person-to-person evaluation involves comparing how well each salesperson has done over a given period. Current-to-past evaluation involves comparing for each individual salesperson the sales they have achieved this month as against last month, or possibly this month compared with the same month last year. Regardless of which way you go about it, the object of the exercise is to highlight good or bad performance, but you need to be sensible about how you use this kind of information. There may be good reasons why the performance of a particular salesperson during a particular month has not been terribly impressive. You should take the trouble to find out what has caused the poor performance before you start waving a big stick. Again you must remember to praise especially good performance with an enthusiasm at least equal to your condemnation of poor performance.

Several other performance indicators are available and are widely used in large firms. These involve working out ratios of one kind or another and keeping track of how they change over time. They include:
- average number of sales visits per rep per week
- productive calls (i.e. those which result in an order) as a percentage of total calls
- cost per call
- cost per order

Most small firms do not have the time to go into this kind of detail at least in the early stages of their development. However it may be useful to do a rough sum now and again. You might discover, for example, that some orders are costing more to obtain than they yield in terms of profits.

SELLING THROUGH AN AGENT OR DISTRIBUTOR
This is your third alternative way of selling your product or service. It has already been discussed in some detail in Chapter 6. Just remember that you will still have to sell your company and products to an agent or distributor in the first place, and subsequently keep in close and regular touch to make sure that a good job is being done for you.

Summary of Key Points
1. Employing a salesperson is a big step for any small firm, but an essential one if the business is to expand. Sooner or later, you will reach the point where it is not longer physically possible for you to follow up all the sales leads coming forward.
2. Employing sales people will present a whole new set of management tasks for you to handle, including recruitment, training, motivation, organisation and control.
3. You need to be clear in your own mind about what kind of sales people you require, and what tasks you want them to perform, before you start recruiting. A job analysis and a detailed job description are useful aids.
4. Regardless of how experienced a salesperson is, he or she will need some additional training. As a minimum, they will require a full briefing of your current product range, customer needs, competitors' activities, and company policies and procedures.
5. The right level of remuneration is crucial in recruiting and retaining good sales staff. A very wide range of different remuneration packages has been devised, the most common being a basic salary plus commission on sales above a certain level.
6. Financial rewards are not the only, or necessarily even the best way to motivate sales staff. Encouragement and support, and a clear recognition of their efforts are of at least equal importance.
7. It is essential to organise and control the activities of your sales staff so as to make the most effective use of their valuable time. This will involve a clear definition of sales territories, accurate records, regular meetings and evaluation of their performance.

A Case History
During the early 1970s, a small firm in Northern Ireland which supplied and fitted plate glass shop windows found it was paying its sales people substantially more than the managing director and about three or four times as much as any other employee. It is not hard to imagine the ten-

sions and resentments which resulted from that situation. The problem arose because the demand for replacement shop fronts reached unprecedented levels as a direct result of the Province's political troubles. It was made worse because of the firm's contractual obligation to pay a specified level of commission on all sales, and was only resolved after lengthy and difficult negotiations to make the scheme more flexible.

11.
Developing a Marketing Strategy

You may think it is a totally ridiculous that a small firm should have to bother with grand notions such as developing a marketing strategy. That kind of thing is all very well for Guinness or Jefferson-Smurfit — it is not really necessary, or even possible, you may think, for a company the size of yours. But hold on a minute. You must surely be working to some kind of game plan, some vague notion of how you see the business developing over the next couple of years or so. Otherwise, how can you possibly make sensible decisions about buying equipment, taking on more staff and so on? The chances are that you are already working to a basic strategy, even though you may not have thought it through in detail. The purpose of this chapter is to provide some guidelines which will help you to do so. You will find it useful to look at three separate issues in turn:

- What is meant by the term 'Marketing Strategy'?
- What strategic alternatives are available to the small firm?
- What are the main steps involved in developing a marketing strategy?

THE COMPONENTS OF A MARKETING STRATEGY

The first thing you have to realise is that a company's marketing strategy is part of its overall corporate strategy. You cannot have a meaningful marketing strategy without reference to the overall corporate strategy. A company's corporate strategy is a statement which looks ahead for a relatively long period of time (five to ten years), and sets out:

- where the company wants to go, and
- how it intends to get there.

A company's strategic objectives (i.e. where it wants to go) are defined in terms of things such as:

- the scope and range of its activities
- the overall size and location of its operations
- target levels of sales and profitability

Developing a Marketing Strategy

How it intends to get there is expressed in terms of major policies and programmes of action including, for example, anticipated levels of investment.

A company's corporate strategy is determined by:
- its expectations regarding future conditions and trends in the business environment;
- its internal strengths and weaknesses, and the resources likely to be available;
- the personal values of its managers.

The first two of these will determine what is possible; the third factor comes into play in deciding which of a number of different possible courses of action is felt to be desirable. For instance a company in the tobacco industry may come to the conclusion that its long term outlook is poor because of changing attitudes to smoking and health. Thus its main strategic objective might be to diversify into other areas of commercial activity which offer better prospects for survival and profitability in the years ahead. A wide range of possible diversification opportunities may be apparent, but not all of these will be feasible in terms of the resources available. The final choice of which option the company actively pursues will be made by the Board of Directors and its senior managers. These people will inevitably be influenced by their own attitudes, prejudices, previous experience, and moral and ethical values.

In the same way as this hypothetical tobacco company, you need to sort out your corporate objectives before you get down to devising a marketing strategy. Looking ten years down the road, what is the ideal situation you can foresee for your business and for you personally? Do you want to be a millionaire? Or would you be happy with a business which provides a decent living for yourself and your family? Do you want to pass on a sound, viable business to your children? Or do you intend to sell it off and retire somewhere nice on the proceeds? To put these issues in a more formalised way, a small firm can pursue a number of radically different long-term corporate objectives, including:
- rapid growth
- slow, steady growth
- survival at more or less its present size

Your decision on which of these objectives you are aiming for (or indeed any other objectives you care to define) will strongly influence your marketing strategy.

A statement outlining a company's marketing strategy will address, in relation to its marketing activities, the two fundamental questions set out above — i.e. where it is going and how it intends to get there. Answering these questions in marketing terms will require decisions about:

- which markets or market segments it intends to service;
- on what basis the company will compete within these markets;
- what it hopes to achieve in sales and profitability.

Market segmentation, the process of sub-dividing a market into smaller sub-groups, was discussed in some detail in Chapter 2. Perhaps the most basic marketing decision you will have to make is whether to aim at covering the total market for your particular product or service (sometimes referred to as 'mass' marketing), or to concentrate your efforts on one or two specific segments within it ('niche' marketing). You will also have to decide the extent of the geographical area in which you propose to operate and whether or not you intend to broaden the scope of your activities in the foreseeable future by offering different products and services.

Another key decision area concerns the positioning of your product or service in relation to those of your competitors. How do you want your company to be perceived by potential customers when they compare the price and quality of the various alternatives on offer? How do you intend to make sure that you are getting across the right message to them, and that your products will be available wherever and whenever your customers want to buy them? Your marketing strategy should also include statements about the broad policies you intend to apply in respect of:

- the range of products or services to be offered
- the quality to be maintained
- the introduction of new products or services
- your approach to pricing
- your approach to advertising and sales promotion
- distribution arrangements

ALTERNATIVE MARKETING STRATEGIES FOR THE SMALL FIRM

People who run small firms are reminded every other day of their social obligation to expand, thereby creating some badly-needed jobs. These exhortations usually come from politicians, civil servants and academics — from people who do not have to to face up to the stresses and strains involved in managing a small business. Perhaps they need to be reminded that a perfectly respectable strategic objective for any small firm is to remain small, yielding a net return sufficient to provide a decent living for the owner/manager and his or her family.

Developing a Marketing Strategy 175

The main advantage of remaining small is that the whole enterprise can be kept within manageable limits. There are literally thousands of small firms throughout the country which have managed to survive and remain viable over quite a long period of time — several generations, in some cases. If you look at the strategy which has enabled them to do so, you will see that in nearly every case, they have identified their own particular niche within a much larger market. Quite often this niche can be defined geographically — the only supplier of such-and-such a product or service in the county, or in the east end of the city. Sometimes the niche needs to be defined in terms of serving the needs of a particular highly-specialised group of customers. Believe it or not, there is in the North a small firm which specialises in painting banners for Orange Lodges.

However there are also some disadvantages associated with remaining small. A small, independent company is extremely vulnerable. It can be put out of business overnight by factors completely beyond its control. Every time a large firm closes down, you can rest assured that a number of its smaller suppliers, and small firms servicing the needs of its employees, will have suffered the same fate. A small manufacturer is easily overwhelmed by the sudden appearance of a flood of cheap but good-quality imports. Complacency is the greatest single risk factor. There is an enormous temptation for the owner/manager who has enjoyed a long period of reasonably profitable stability to assume that this desirable state of affairs will continue indefinitely. It may turn out like that — but you have to work at it. The only prediction you can make with absolute certainty is that the future will be different from the present. A deliberate decision to opt for a quieter life by remaining small does not imply that it is safe to fall asleep! You still need to be alive to changing customer needs and competitive activity. You still need to adapt the products or services you offer to meet these changes and to communicate effectively with customers. You still need to be clear about your long-term objectives. For instance, what do you intend should happen to the business when you eventually become too old and tired to run it effectively? Do you intend to sell it? If so, to whom, and for how much, and how are you going to structure it so as to get the best possible price? Do you intend to pass it on to your children? If so, what plans have you made to train them and ensure a smooth transition when you finally let go of the reins? You still need to work out a long-term strategy which will provide guidelines for your day-to-day management decisions.

On the other hand, you may well decide to go for growth. If you do, a wide range of strategic marketing options is open to you. These include:

- market penetration
- market development
- product development
- diversification
- acquisition

Market Penetration

The most straightforward path to growth is to aim at increasing the sales of your current product range within those markets you already service. In order to do this, you will have to:

- persuade some of your competitors' customers to switch over to you;
- persuade your own customers to buy more; or
- persuade people who have not previously used this product or service to start doing so.

Market Development

An alternative way forward is to develop new markets for your products. This can be done by expanding the scope of your activities into new geographical areas, or by moving into new segments of the total market within the geographical area in which you currently operate.

Product Development

A third alternative is to expand by developing new products or services which you can offer to your existing customers. This does not necessarily mean spending a fortune in discovering and perfecting a major technological breakthrough. A 'new' product may be a relatively minor modification of an existing one (see Chapter 4).

Diversification

Diversification implies moving into an area of business which is radically different from what you are doing at present. It is not an easy option because it involves learning a whole new set of tricks in a very short period of time. As a general rule, it should only be considered by a small firm which is completely on top of its existing activities, and when the diversification opportunity is really attractive. Trying to bite off more than you can chew is usually a recipe for disaster.

Acquisition

Acquisitions and mergers are not the sole preserve of the major multinationals. There are many examples of small firms which have grown

Developing a Marketing Strategy 177

very big very quickly by following this strategy. It requires a lot of skillful management, and is not recommended unless you really know what you are doing. It also frequently involves some loss of ownership and control of the business, in that external sources of funds are usually required. Nevertheless it is a strategy worth considering if your objective is to achieve rapid growth.

Some of the risks

There is no doubt that developing a small business successfully is an effective way of becoming very well off, perhaps even rich. But you should also be aware of the risks involved. Many small firms go under as a result of over-trading. In simple terms, this means running out of cash by expanding too quickly. A typical scenario would be where a small firm obtains a large number of new orders, takes on extra staff and buys the materials needed to meet them and then discovers that these bills have to be paid before the money has come in. Your bank manager may be sympathetic to this kind of problem — but don't count on it. Prudent financial management is an essential ingredient in your overall marketing strategy.

Another common cause of failure is the inability of the person who starts up a small firm to recognise the point at which additional management expertise is required. Sooner or later as the business expands, the number, range and complexity of management tasks that need to be done will become too much for a single person to handle. Disaster is inevitable unless extra help is brought on board. This particular problem often occurs in the area of sales and marketing. A typical situation is where the founder of the business is an engineer or an accountant with limited knowledge of marketing. In the early stages of growth, it is possible to survive by relying on native wit and a minimum of instruction, buy eventually someone with real expertise and experience in this field will be needed.

Finally, the more successful a small business becomes, the more likely it is to attract the attention of its larger competitors. The outcome may be a take-over bid which is not necessarily a bad thing. Rather than face the prospect of a prolonged battle which you may not win, you may decide it is wiser to take the money and run. You can then use your capital to start another business, or else retire gracefully from the scene if you have had enough. A more unpleasant possibility is that they may try to force you out of business by exerting the maximum competitive pressure they can muster. One way of avoiding this is to adopt a 'multiple niche' strategy — i.e. to concentrate your activities in a number of areas which are too small or too specialised for the big boys to bother about. You should reflect on the fact that many of the most successful small firms around at the moment have survived and prospered by taking this approach.

THE STEPS INVOLVED IN DEVELOPING A MARKETING STRATEGY

Effective marketing requires flair and imagination and a bit of showmanship — but it also requires a lot of thought and careful preparation. Developing a sound, long-term marketing strategy is one of those areas where perspiration is at least as important as inspiration. There is a logical sequence of steps involved in thinking it through. You need to:

- analyse opportunities and threats in the market
- evaluate the company's strengths and weaknesses
- set specific marketing objectives
- develop alternative strategies for achieving those objectives
- decide which strategy is most likely to be successful
- take positive steps to implement your chosen strategy

Market Analysis

You need to have a clear picture of where your company stands at the moment before you start making statements about where you want it to be in five years' time. Your starting point should be a careful analysis of what is happening in the markets you service in terms of:

- customer needs
- competitive activity

The most basic question you have to answer is whether the demand for products or services of the kind you provide is likely to increase, decrease or remain more or less static in the immediate future. It is totally unrealistic for you to think in terms of developing your own detailed forecast of market trends. But you may well be able to pick up some information of this kind prepared by government departments, trade associations and so on. Your own knowledge of customer needs, supplemented by material you may come across (for example in trade journals), should enable you to speculate about how their needs and tastes are likely to change in the years ahead. You need to subdivide the market into its various segments and look at each of them separately. You also need to make guesses about how your competitors may react and about the strength of the competitors you are likely to face. Of course all of this presupposes that you have done some basic market research in the first place. If you haven't, you would need to get onto it right away. It is simply not possible to make sensible decisions without some basic market knowledge. However, you should also realise that you are very unlikely to be able to find out absolutely everything you want to know. It is equally unrealistic to postpone making any decisions until you have reached a state of perfect knowledge. You will have to make educated guesses about the way things are likely to go. Just remember there is a world of difference between a pure guess pulled out of the air and based on nothing more substantial than hope, and sensible speculation based on your own expert opinion, backed up by some hard facts and a lot of experience. The outcome of your market analysis should be a clear statement of the opportunities and threats you are likely to encounter in the years ahead.

Company Evaluation

Having looked at the external factors which may present opportunities and threats to your company, you then need to look inwards and make an assessment of its strengths and weaknesses. Your appraisal has to be objective and realistic — there is no point kidding yourself that things are better (or worse) than they actually are. You must deal with the world as it is, which is not necessarily the same as how you would like it to be. You need to look at the financial, technical and human resources which are available at present and which are likely to be available in the future. Depending on the nature of your own particular business, this will raise many detailed questions, including:

- Is your production capacity adequate?
- Is your plant and machinery up-to-date?
- Are your premises big enough, and in the right location?
- Could you finance a modernisation programme and an expansion of the scale of the operation?
- Do you have the right people in the right jobs?
- Could you find more staff of the right calibre if you need them?

The list of possible questions of this kind is not quite endless, but it is certainly very wide ranging. You may think it is unnecessary to do a detailed appraisal of the current state of your business along these lines. But you need to be sure of what it is capable of handling before you make major decisions about its future directions.

Setting Marketing Objectives

The next step is to formulate your long-term marketing objectives. These are normally expressed in terms of:

- the markets or market segments in which you propose to operate;
- the products and services you intend to offer, and how they are to be positioned within the market;
- the volume of sales you hope to achieve;
- the level of profit you expect to earn.

Each of these broad headings may include a number of subsidiary objectives. For instance, you may decide to aim at expanding the scope of your operation into a new market — in which case you will need to consider your timing and method of entry. The objectives you set should be:
- realistic
- achievable
- flexible

Every marketing opportunity has certain success requirements associated with it. Every company is subject to limitations on what it can do at any particular time. It is vitally important to make sure that your company's resources and abilities are capable of meeting the success requirements set by the market at least as well as any existing or potential competitor. If a particular course of action fails to satisfy this key requirement, you will be well advised to back off and try something else, because you are certain to be unsuccessful in the long run. A deliberately ridiculous example may serve to illustrate the point.

A small engineering company based somewhere in the middle of Ireland might conceivably discover that many of the world's oil tankers are nearing the end of their working life, and that there is likely to be a major marketing opportunity for fleet replacement sales throughout the 1990s. That may well be the case — but pursuing this particular opportunity is not a realistic and achievable objective for this particular firm because its resources and abilities are so far removed from what is required to exploit successfully the opportunity it has identified. A marketing opportunity in advanced medical instruments or computer-controlled machine tools is unlikely to be attractive to an airline unless it is pursuing a strategy of diversification through acquisition.

Setting strategic objectives involves making major decisions which have long-term implications for the future of the business. The essential purpose of a marketing strategy is to provide you with a game plan you can work to, and to help you make sensible management decisions within the context of a clear statement of what you are trying to achieve. It is a major mistake to chop and change your so-called 'strategy' every couple of months. But equally, you should not regard a particular strategy as being set immovably in tablets of stone, to be followed slavishly regardless of what is happening in the rest of the world. You will need to reconsider your strategy from time to time, and perhaps revise it as circumstances dictate. In fact, one of the major competitive advantages small firms have over their bigger rivals is their ability to change direction quickly if they have to.

Choosing a Strategy

There is no single, guaranteed 'right' way of achieving a particular set of objectives. There will always be alternatives, each of which will offer its own costs and benefits. For instance, a company can try to enter a new market by allocating one of its sales people to develop it. The main advantage is that an existing employee will already have acquired a lot of product and customer knowledge. The main disadvantage is that he or she will have less time to spend on their current activities and sales may suffer as a result. An alternative approach would be to employ an additional salesperson. This might involve living with a substantial negative cash flow before new business starts to come on-stream, but on the other hand the existing customer base would not suffer. A third approach would be to sell through an agent or distributor. This might be an easy way to make contact with a large number of potential new customers, but inevitably some revenue would be lost in commission payments.

Many small firms make the mistake of not thinking through the possible alternatives in this kind of way and simply opt for the first solution that springs to mind. It is always worthwhile to at least consider the alternatives, even though you might end up choosing the one you thought of in the first place. You should choose the approach which is most likely to achieve your objectives, having weighed up the costs and benefits associated with each of the alternatives you have identified. Unfortunately it is not possible to provide more detailed guidance on this point because every firm and every market is different. This is one more area where you will have to come up with solutions which are specific to your own situation. You may find it useful to try to write down the alternative approaches it would be possible for you to take in respect of the four main areas of marketing activity — the range of products and services to be offered, pricing, advertising and sales promotion, and distribution. Remember that your choices in these four areas must not contradict each other. They should fit together as a coherent total approach to the achievement of your objectives.

Implementation

There is no point whatsoever in taking the trouble to develop a marketing strategy unless you take positive action to implement it. You need to direct your firm's marketing activities on a day-to-day and month-to-month basis. In other words, you also need a marketing plan.

Summary of Key Points

1. A marketing strategy is a statement of where the company is going and how it intends to get there. This will involve making decisions about which markets or market segments it will operate in, and what it hopes to achieve in terms of sales and profitability. Another key decision area is the positioning of your product or service in relation to those of your competitors.
2. Your personal values and aspirations are also important. A deliberate decision to remain small and easier to manage may be attractive, but there are risks associated with this strategy. If you go for growth, a number of strategic options are available. These include market penetration, market development, product development, diversification and acquisition.
3. There is a logical sequence of steps involved in developing a marketing strategy. The starting point is a careful analysis of future opportunities and threats in the market you wish to compete in, and an evaluation of your company's internal strengths and weaknesses.
4. The next step is to formulate long-term marketing objectives. These should be realistic and quantified as far as possible. They should also be flexible enough to allow you to adapt to unforeseen circumstances.
5. There is no single guaranteed 'right' way of achieving a particular set of objectives. There will always be alternatives, each of which will offer its own costs and benefits. It is always worthwhile considering the alternatives rather than simply opting for the first solution that springs to mind.
6. There is no point in developing a long-term marketing strategy unless you take positive steps to implement it.

12.
Drawing up a Marketing Plan

Many small firms do not have any kind of marketing plan. This is mainly due to the fact that the people responsible for managing small firms have no idea of what a marketing plan should look like, or how to go about drawing one up. Some of them seem to think that a marketing plan has to be a lengthy and complicated document at least two inches thick. That is quite possibly true in the case of a company the size of Ford or IBM, but a perfectly adequate marketing plan for a small firm can be presented on three or four pages. There are at least two good reasons why every small firm should go to the trouble of preparing one. First, you will almost certainly be asked to produce it for discussion when you approach your bank manager for additional funding, or a government agency for grant aid or some other kind of support. Secondly, a marketing plan is an essential component in your overall approach to the management of your business. It is a vitally important control mechanism. If you don't know what is supposed to be happening in terms of your marketing activities, how can you be sure that what is actually happening on a day-to-day and month-by-month basis makes sense in the context of the long-term development of your firm? Or even in the more immediately urgent context of generating a sufficient volume of sales to avoid going bust. Some of the confusion about drawing up a marketing plan can be cleared up by thinking about what is normally meant by the words 'plan' and 'planning' in other situations.

The plan of a building will show you the size and shape of the various rooms it contains and how they fit together. A marketing plan performs the same basic functions. It outlines the size and shape of the various different aspects of the firm's overall marketing activities and brings them together into a coherent and meaningful whole. A building can be planned well or badly and as a result it can be a great success, just about adequate, or a total failure. In exactly the same way, the success or otherwise of your marketing efforts will depend largely on how well you have planned them.

In a slightly different sense, planning can be defined as deciding in the present what to do in the future. Forward planning takes place at many different levels and in relation to different periods of time. At one level, the government plans a long-term economic strategy for the whole country (or so they say). At another level, a housewife plans her purchases in the supermarket so that she can feed her family during the week ahead. In business, marketing planning takes place at three different levels and time periods:

- long-term strategic planning
- short-term tactical planning
- detailed activity planning

Your long-term marketing strategy will set out in broad terms where you intend to go over the next five years or so. You then need to refine this by setting out in some detail what action you propose to take in the immediate future. This is normally taken to mean during the next twelve months. The annual marketing plan spells out a specific programme of activities aimed at achieving limited short-term objectives — i.e. with making some progress down the road towards the ultimate goals set out in the long-term marketing strategy. Referring to this as 'tactical' as opposed to 'strategic' planning sometimes causes great confusion. The annual marketing plan is prepared within the broad policy guidelines which together comprise a company's marketing strategy. It is usually possible to come up with a number of different ways of implementing this strategy. Decisions on which short-term courses of action are to be followed are decisions about marketing tactics. If the basic policy guidelines are adhered to, then the underlying strategy remains unaffected by the tactical choices that have been made. Some examples of the strategic and tactical decisions which might be made by a small firm are shown in Figure 12.

To complete the planning process, some of the activities specified in the annual marketing plan may require a separate detailed plan of how and when they are to be implemented. For example, organising an advertising campaign would involve specifying the dates by which certain key tasks must be completed. In larger firms, management techniques such as Critical Path Analysis are often used for this purpose. There is no reason at all why a smaller firm should not do so as well if the necessary expertise is available.

Drawing up an annual marketing plan for a small firm involves:

- setting sales targets
- specifying the activities required to achieve them
- allocating the resources needed

Figure 12. Strategy and Tactics (Manufacturer of Household Paint)

	Strategic Decision	*Tactical Decisions*
Target Market	Aim to cover all market segments or concentrate solely on industrial sector	Identify key accounts in each segment
Product Range	Offer widest possible range of colours in 3-pack sizes	Alter range of colours in accordance with the pattern of demand. Re-design packaging
Promotion	Maintain high quality image	Change advertising themes regularly. Print new catalogue
Price	Maintain a premium price 10% above main competitor	Amend prices in line with inflation. Negotiate bulk-purchase discounts. Run special offers
Distribution	Maximise number of retail outlets	Add/remove stockists as required

SETTING SALES TARGETS

Many large firms use sophisticated statistical techniques to develop industry-wide forecasts of future sales. They then estimate the share of the market they are likely to achieve in different circumstances, using computer-based models to explore a wide range of alternative scenarios. This approach is not feasible for the average small firm, which is unlikely to have either the time or the expertise required. Nor is it particularly helpful for a small firm to know that its market share will probably be around .01 per cent. At the end of the day, the sole purpose of running a small business is to make a profit. Therefore, your absolute minimum target must be to sell enough to cover your costs. Your business will not survive for long if you do not at least achieve that objective. At the other end of the spectrum, your existing plant and equipment will set a limit on your total output. The only pos-sible way you can sell more than this is by quoting longer and longer delivery times. Sooner or later, some of your customers will not be prepared to put up with the inevitable delays and will go elsewhere.

You can set your sales target at any level you like in between these two extremes. It is really a question of using your judgment to home in on a target which, in your opinion:

- is attainable
- will yield what you would consider to be an acceptable return

As a general rule, higher sales means higher profits, but profit margins may vary at different levels of output. You need to know the relationship between sales volume and profitability, and how the figures on the bottom line will change as sales increase or decrease. There is absolutely no point in achieving a very high volume of unprofitable sales — that is why the easy option of 'buying' additional sales by reducing your price and sacrificing profit should only be taken as a last resort. The baseline most firms use for setting sales targets is their actual performance during the current and previous years. This is a useful starting point, but it is a mistake to simply add on ten per cent, or some other figure pulled out of the air. That is far too simplistic. An automatic annual increase in sales for every product in every sales territory is by no means guaranteed.

You need to make a fresh assessment of your prospects, taking into account as best you can the market conditions you foresee. Perfect knowledge of the future state of the world is not currently available to the average small firm, so you will have to make some assumptions about what is likely to happen over the next twelve months. What will the economy be like? What are your competitors going to do? What other assumptions are you making? A useful approach is to estimate first of all how much of a particular product you reckon can be sold based on fairly optimistic (but realistic) assumptions. Then repeat the exercise, this time making more pessimistic assumptions. Then split the difference to arrive at a target which you believe is realistic and achievable. The next step is to calculate how much profit will accrue from that level of sales. If the answer is 'not enough', you will need to think again. Can you make up the short-fall from sales of other products? Can you improve your profitability by reducing your costs, or by increasing your price, or a little bit of both?

Drawing up a Marketing Plan 187

The whole point of taking this approach is that it starts by looking at the market and then works backwards from there. This is the reverse of the approach normally followed by your accountant, who will take as his or her starting point the amount of profit he or she feels is required to provide an adequate return on the capital invested in the business. Your accountant will then look at your costs and calculate the volume of sales required to attain the profit target he/she has in mind for you. This is, of course, a very sensible way to proceed. The only problem is that it may not take full account of what is happening out there in the market place — and it is these external factors which will decide whether or not a particular target is attainable. You need to balance the requirements set by your accountant against your own assessment of market conditions before you finally agree a specific target for total annual sales of each of the products or services you provide. Having done that, you will then need to break down your annual targets into monthly targets, making allowances as appropriate for seasonal fluctuations, holiday periods and so on.

This procedure is relatively straightforward in the case of a one-product company operating in a clearly defined geographical area. The arithmetic is more complicated if you have a number of products sold in a number of different areas, but the basic principles remain the same. The easiest way to deal with the problem is to do your sums separately for each product in each area. You can then use these figures to build up an overall total picture. What emerges may not be to your liking. For instance, you may find that the target set for total sales of all products in a particular territory is impossibly high, or that the predicted final net profit for the business as a whole is too low. If that should happen, go over your figures again until you come up with a series of targets which you can accept as being attainable and also capable of yielding the level of profit you require.

You may have been expecting to read about some simple formula which can be used to set sales targets in any small firm. Unfortunately, no such thing exists. If you feel the approach outlined above is a little bit haphazard and subjective, just remember that the most sophisticated computer model used by a major multinational company also relies on the subjective judgment of the people using it. They will have made certain assumptions about market trends and competitive activities — and they are just as likely as you are to get it wrong. Setting sales targets is not an exact science. It is rather a question of applying your experience and knowledge of the market to your calculations of the relationship between sales revenue, costs and profit contribution at different levels of output.

SPECIFYING ACTIVITIES

Once you have set yourself a series of sales targets, you need to give some careful thought to how you are going to set about the task of achieving them. A certain amount of optimistic enthusiasm is very necessary. But you will have to spell out in some detail what exactly you are going to do in the way of advertising, sales promotion, publicity material and so on. You will also have to plan the timing and sequence of these various activities over the year ahead in order to achieve the maximum impact in support of your efforts to generate sales. For instance, you may decide to take a stand at a trade fair or exhibition, or to run a major advertising campaign in late November/early December to make sure of getting your share of the traditional pre-Christmas surge in demand. Here again, only you can decide what specific activities are appropriate to your particular situation.

ALLOCATING RESOURCES

The final stage in preparing an annual marketing plan is to allocate sufficient resources to enable you to implement it properly. You will need to cost out as accurately as you can the activities you plan to undertake and draw up a marketing budget showing your projected expenditure on a monthly basis. This will, of course, appear as a cost item in your overall cash flow projections. But remember that it is just as much an investment in the future of your company as buying a new machine or refurbishing your premises. The biggest single mistake you can make at this stage is to make the false economy of cutting back on the marketing budget because the sums don't quite add up as you would like for the business as a whole. Look for economies and cost savings elsewhere — there is bound to be some slack somewhere. There is a direct relationship between your expenditure on marketing and achieving your sales target. Sometimes the precise nature of that relationship is not entirely clear. You can spend a given amount of money wisely and to great effect, or unwisely and achieve virtually nothing. Nevertheless the link does exist.

The one thing you must not do is to try and implement the marketing programme you have planned on a budget which is insufficient to allow you do so effectively. If you simply cannot afford it, the most sensible thing to do is to go back to the drawing board, revise your objectives and come up with a more modest plan which you can fund. (See Chapter 7 'How much to spend'.)

Drawing up a Marketing Plan

THE LAY-OUT OF A MARKETING PLAN

There is no generally accepted right way of setting out a marketing plan in a format which you can show to your fellow directors or your bank manager. As an absolute minimum, the simplest marketing plan should contain:

- a table showing how much of each product you expect to sell each month of the year ahead;
- an accompanying statement setting out the nature and timing of the various marketing activities you propose to undertake to help you achieve these targets;
- a budget showing the amount of money available to carry out the tasks you have specified.

A more comprehensive marketing plan might be presented along the lines shown in Figure 13.

Figure 13. ABC Enterprise Ltd, Marketing Plan for 1992

1. Background
A review of recent performance and current outlook — market trends, changes in customer needs/preferences, competitive activity etc.

2. Objectives
Brief summary of long-term marketing strategy and objectives.
Specific objectives for the next twelve months, including targets for volume and value of sales and net profit contribution for each product and sales territory.

3. Product Policy
Review of the existing product range in comparison with main competitors. Statement of any new product launches (or withdrawals of older products) scheduled for the current year, and any proposed modifications to existing products.

4. Pricing
Review of the existing price structure in comparison with main competitors. Summary of any anticipated changes in materials, manufacturing, distribution, or other costs likely to erode or improve profit margins.

Statement of policy to be adopted if anticipated changes in cost structure actually occur: e.g. absorb higher costs within existing prices or alternatively maintain gross margins by raising prices if necessary.

Statement of anticipated changes in pricing policy of major competitors, and of how the company will respond if these occur.

5. Distribution Arrangements

Comment on whether or not existing arrangements are satisfactory. Proposed changes and reasons for changing: i.e. number and type of outlets serviced, number and location of storage/warehouse facilities, transport.

6. Advertising and Sales Promotion

Total expenditure proposed; changes as compared with current year; reasons for change. Summary of promotional approach to be used: i.e. target audience, main messages to be communicated etc.

Allocation of total budget between media alternative, e.g.

	£'000
Television	25
National press	10
Local press	8
Publicity material	7
	50

Allocation of expenditure over time: i.e. a schedule showing when specific events are planned to take place.

7. Sales

Proposed changes in size or role of sales force and rationale for proposed changes. Proposed staff development or training activities.

Projected costs of sales force, by sales territory and in total.

	Area A	Area B	Area C	Total
		(£'000s)		
Salaries				
Commission				
Expenses				
Vehicles				
Sales Aids				
TOTAL				

Targets for total sales by product and area:

	Area A % 1990 1991 change	Area B % 1990 1991 change	Area C % 1990 1991 change	Total % 1990 1991 change
Product A				
Product B				
Product C				
Product D	— — —	— — —	— — —	— — —

KEEPING THINGS UNDER CONTROL

A detailed marketing plan along these lines is very useful for convincing others that you know what you are doing, but its basic purpose is to make sure *you* know what you are doing. Annual targets for sales, costs and profits can readily be converted into monthly targets, making appropriate allowance for seasonal fluctuations. Using modern computer technology (a number of standard software packages is available), you can obtain at the end of each month a full report comparing actual performance against target (see Figure 14). This will provide you with an early warning of where things might be going wrong, and hopefully enable you to take prompt corrective action before the situation gets out of hand.

Figure 14. ABC Enterprise Ltd, Monthly Sales Report—Area A

	Month – October			Year to date		
	Target	Actual	Variance (%)	Target	Actual	Variance (%)
Product A						
Product B						
Product C						
Product D	___	___	___	___	___	___
Total Sales						
Cost of Sales						
Profit						
Contribution						

Summary of Key Points

1. A marketing plan is an essential component in the management of your business. It is a vitally important control mechanism. It should specify in detail the various different aspects of the firm's overall marketing activities and bring them together into a coherent programme of action.
2. Marketing planning takes place at three different levels. Your long-term strategy will set out in broad terms where you want to go over the next three to five years. Your annual marketing plan will specify in detail what you propose to do over the next twelve months. Finally, some of the activities specified in the annual marketing plan (e.g. an advertising campaign) may require a separate and detailed plan of how and when they are to be implemented.
3. Drawing up an annual marketing plan involves setting sales targets, specifying the activities needed to achieve them and allocating the resources needed.
4. Your absolute minimum target must be to sell enough to cover your costs, including a living wage for yourself. Beyond that, it is a question of using your judgement to set a target which is attainable and will yield an acceptable level of profit.
5. Once you have set yourself a series of sales targets, you need to specify in detail what exactly you are going to do in the way of advertising, sales promotion, publicity material and so on in order to achieve them. You will also have to plan the timing and sequence of these activities.
6. The final stage is to cost out the activities you propose to undertake and draw up a marketing budget showing your projected expenditure each month and in total.
7. There is no generally accepted 'right' way of setting out a marketing plan similar to the standard format of a set of accounts. The important thing is that your marketing plan should be presented clearly in a format which can easily understood by your fellow directors and by your bank manager.

13.
The Way Ahead

During the 1990s we can be fairly certain that the competitive pressures faced by small firms in Ireland will become even more intense. If they are to survive and prosper, it is absolutely essential that they get their act together and keep in good shape to face up to the challenges which lie ahead. This implies making the fullest possible use of modern technology to remain competitive in production, taking care to ensure that they have well-trained, highly-motivated staff, and a sound financial structure. But effective marketing will continue to be a vital success requirement. This book has covered a lot of ground and hopefully will provide a useful point of reference on the nuts and bolts of practical marketing which the reader can dip into from time to time as the need arises. However, the fundamental message it has tried to get across is that successful marketing is not simply a question of good luck and natural flair; it is more likely to be the result of careful analysis and the imaginative implementation of a well thought-out long-term strategy. It could be argued that the basic ingredients for marketing success are:

- Information
- Imagination
- Implementation

INFORMATION

In this modern rapidly-changing world, it is of crucial importance that you keep up-to-date with what is happening around you. Opportunities and threats are emerging all the time and you need to be ready to react appropriately as the need arises. Accurate knowledge of the changing scene out there in the market should be the basis for all your marketing decisions. The influence of market trends — the tastes, preferences, attitudes and needs of your customers and the activities of your competitors — should be clearly seen in the way you adapt your product range, your pricing policy, and your approach to advertising, sales promotion and distribution. You also need detailed and accurate information about what is happening within the firm. You need to know in detail the costs and profitability of each item in your product range and how these will be affected by changes in volume, or in the price of your raw materials, or whatever. You need to have a clear idea of the cost-effectiveness of your advertising and sales activities, and of your distribution arrangements. Only then will you be in a position to make informed decisions and plan ahead within clearly-defined parameters.

IMAGINATION

Someone once said that a board of directors composed entirely of accountants is a bit like a football team made up entirely of goalkeepers. Some people (especially accountants) would regard that as a vile insult against an honourable body of men and women, and in all fairness it is something of a caricature. Nevertheless the basic point implied in that remark is still valid. Every successful company needs somebody who has the imagination and flair needed to score the winning goal. But imagination and flair should not be taken to simply mean indulging in wild flights of fancy, impossible dreams — this year we'll consolidate our market share in West Cork; next year we'll go into Europe, and the year after that we'll conquer America! A solid dose of pragmatic realism will always be needed.

In a marketing context, imagination means having sufficient foresight to see that the game is changing, and the vision and flexibility which is needed to change direction quickly and, perhaps, radically. Imagination implies a willingness to innovate, an openness to new ideas and approaches to product development and sales promotion alike, an ability to see your company and its products from the customer's point of view rather than your own. Imagination also implies creativity and flair in product design, advertising and distribution — or at least the ability to recognise and utilise creative flair in others if you do not possess it yourself.

IMPLEMENTATION

Collecting information and using it imaginatively is all very well, but your success or failure will ultimately be decided by what you actually do with your business from day to day. Effective implementation does not mean simply working very hard, although that will almost certainly be required. It implies planning well in advance what you are going to do and how you are going to do it. It implies organising the human and financial resources available to you in order to maximise your chances of achieving attention to detail and keeping control of every aspect of your firm's activities. In other words, it means being a good manager.

In one sense, successful marketing is an immensely complicated phenomenon which is still not completely understood. Academics have been debating for years exactly how it works, and they have not yet succeeded in coming up with entirely satisfactory answers in a number of areas. Yet in another sense, successful marketing is simply applied common sense. Find out what your customers want and offer it to them at a price they can afford and which will yield you a satisfactory return on the time and money you have invested. If you are unable to do so profitably, try something else.

I wish you every success.

Index

ACORN system, 13-14
acquisitions, 176-7
advertising, 4, 104, 121-42
    costs of, 125-6
    effectiveness of, 29, 134-6
    frequency of, 133-4
    mechanics of, 132-3
    media for, 122-30
    purpose of, 122
    types of, 130-33
    using an agency, 136-41
advertising agencies, 136-41
    choice of, 139-41
    costs of, 138-9
after-sales service, 5
agent
    selling through, 170
agents
    agreements with, 93
    distribution through, 91-4

banks, 34
boutiques, specialist, 88
brainstorming, 56
brand images, 131-2
business environment
    market research into, 29-32
buying signals, 154-5

calendars/diaries, 115
cinema advertisements, 129
cold calling, 148
company evaluation, 179
competition, 18-20
    and advertising, 130
    market research into, 27-8, 33
    and marketing strategy, 174
    and pricing, 65-70
    product comparison, 50-51
    and special promotions, 114
competitive tenders, 18
consumer markets, 13-14
corporate identity, 105-6
costs
    of advertising, 125-6, 132-3, 138-9
    break-even point, 73-4
    of customer contact, 116-17
    of marketing plan, 188, 190
    'over-riders', 87
    and pricing, 70-76
Critical Path Analysis, 184
customer
    concept of, 15-18
    contacting, 100-18
    defining, 100-101
    direct distribution to, 79-82
    intermediate customer, 16
    professional buyers, 17-18
    talking to, 153-4
customers
    contacting
        what to spend, 116-17
    former, 147-8
    holding on to, 155
    identification of, 145-8
    market research into, 24-7
    meeting with, 148-9
    orientation towards, 4
    and pricing, 61-5

department stores, 87-8
directories
    advertising in, 129
distribution, 170
    direct to customer, 79-82
    organising, 78-99
    physical logistics, 94-7
    through agents, 91-4
    through wholesalers, 89-91
distribution system, 4-5
diversification, 176
DIY superstores, 88

economy
    effects of, 29-30
European Community (EC), 32
exhibitions, 111-13, 141

Ford, Henry, 2
franchising, 89, 93-4

government departments, 34

health, interest in, 31-2

imagination, 194
implementation, 194-5
industrial markets, 14
information, 193-4
intermediary
    disadvantages of, 83-5
    distribution through, 82-94
    types of, 85-94
interviewing, 160-61
Irish Management Institute, 103

launches, 53, 58-9, 104
legal changes
    effects of, 32
list system, 18

magazine advertisements, 127-9, 133
mail order, 81-2
mail shots, 109-11
mailing list, 111

market, defining of, 11-12
market analysis, 178-9
market development, 176
market penetration, 176
market research, 4, 13, 23-43
    commissioning, 37-40
    on competition, 20
    costs of, 40
    definition of, 24
    of own performance, 28-9
    problems to avoid, 36-7
    techniques of, 32-7
    using the information, 40-41
market segmentation, 12-14, 174
    purpose of, 14-15
market share, building, 67
market testing, 58
marketing
    activities involved, 3-5
    activities of, 8-10
    definition, 5
    future planning, 193-5
    investment in, 7
    market-oriented, 2-3
    mistakes, 5-8
    product-oriented, 1-2
marketing consultants, 140
marketing plan, 5, 182, 183-92
    allocating resources, 188
    keeping under control, 191
    lay-out of, 189-91
    specifying activities, 188
marketing strategy
    alternative, 174-8
    choice of, 181
    components of, 172-4
    developing, 172-82
    setting objectives, 179-81
    steps in developing, 178-82
mass marketing, 174
mergers, 176-7
middleman. *see* intermediary
multiple niche strategy, 177-8
multiple stores, 86-7

newspaper advertisements, 127-9, 132-3
niche marketing, 69-70, 174
non-price factors, 25-6

O'Reilly, A J F, 103
outdoor advertising, 129

packaging, 94-5
party plan distribution, 82
persuasion, 103
political changes
    effects of, 32
price cutting, 67
pricing, 4, 61-77
    contribution approach, 74-6
    effect of price changes, 64-5
    high-price strategy, 68, 70
    and marketing plan, 189
product
    choice of, 4
    deciding on, 44-60
    definition of, 45-7
product development, 176
products
    altering mature product, 54-5
    comparisons of, 48-51
    development of, 55-9
    launching of, 53, 58-9
    life cycle, 51-3
    life-cycle, 54-5
    and marketing plan, 189
    niche product, 69-70
    as opposed to services, 47-8
promotions, special, 113-15
public relations, 115-16, 141
publicity material, 107

quality control, 29

radio advertising, 127
records
    of sales, 168-9
records, need for, 147
recruitment, 158-61

remuneration
    of salespeople, 162-6
reputation, 49-50, 103-4
retail outlets, 80
    as intermediary, 85-9
    'over-riders', 87

sales kit, 151-2
sales management, 157-71
    evaluating performance, 169
    and marketing plan, 190-91
    organisation and control, 166-9
    recruitment, 158-61
    targets, 185-7
    training, 161-6
sales manual, 153
sales presentations, 149-54
sales records, 168-9
sales targets, 168
    setting of, 185-7
sales territories, 166-7
salespeople
    adequate coverage by, 167-8
    evaluating performance of, 169
    remuneration of, 162-6
    women as, 157
samples, 152
selling, 143-56
    closing the sale, 154-5
    identifying customers, 145-8
    as marketing, 4-5
    meeting customers, 148-9
    sales presentations, 149-54
    sales targets, 185-7
services
    as opposed to products, 47-8
    selling of, 145-6
services, marketing of, 4-5
Single European Market, 87
small firms
    marketing strategy for, 174-8
social change
    effects of, 31-2
sponsorship, 115, 129
staff, 159-60

stock-holding, 95
supermarkets
   list system, 17-18

take-over bids, 177
target audience, 101
technology
   effects of changes in, 30-31
television advertising, 123, 126-7, 132
test marketing, 37
trade fairs, 111-13
trade journals, 146-7

training
   of salespeople, 161-6
transportation, 96-7

Unique Selling Proposition (USP) approach, 131

van sales, 80-81
voluntary chain stores, 88-9

wholesalers
   as distributors, 89-91
word-of-mouth, 104-5